Black Money and Tax Evasion in India

Magnitude, Problems and Policy Measures

By

M.M. Sury

New Century Publications
New Delhi, India

NEW CENTURY PUBLICATIONS
4800/24, Bharat Ram Road,
Ansari Road, Daryaganj,
New Delhi – 110 002 (India)

Tel.: 011-2324 7798, 4358 7398, 6539 6605
Fax: 011-4101 7798
E-mail: indiatax@vsnl.com • info@newcenturypublications.com
www.newcenturypublications.com

Editorial office:
LG–7, Aakarshan Bhawan,
4754-57/23, Ansari Road, Daryaganj,
New Delhi – 110 002

Tel.: 011-4356 0919

First Published: **July 2014**

ISBN: **978-81-7708-388-0**

Published by New Century Publications and printed at Salasar Imaging Systems, New Delhi.

Designs: Patch Creative Unit, New Delhi.

PRINTED IN INDIA

About the Book

In recent years, the issue of corruption and black money has come in the forefront after a series of financial scandals. Generation of black money—and its stashing abroad in tax havens and offshore financial centres—has dominated discussions and debate in public fora during the recent past. Members of Parliament, the Supreme Court of India and the public at large have unequivocally expressed concern on the issue, particularly after some reports suggested enormous estimates of such unaccounted wealth being held abroad.

After uproar in Parliament, Government of India came out with a *White Paper* on Black Money in May 2012. The *White Paper* presented the different facets of black money and its complex relationship with policy and administrative regime in the country. It also reflected upon the policy options and strategies that the Government had been pursuing to address the issue of black money and corruption in public life.

To meet the deadline set by the Honourable Supreme Court for the previous Government, the new Government of Prime Minister Narendra Modi constituted a Special Investigation Team (SIT), soon after assuming office on May 26, 2014. Headed by Justice M.B. Shah, a former judge of the Supreme Court, SIT was notified on May 27, 2014 to look into the issue of black money.

The objective of this book is to explain various facets and dimensions of black money and tax evasion and their complex relationship with the policy and administrative regime in the country. It describes the factors which lead to the generation of black money, and records various estimates of black money and tax evasion. It also presents the measures/strategies that the Government of India has been pursuing to tackle this issue, especially recent initiatives and developments.

The work, using simple and non-technical language, is descriptive in nature and designed for a cross section of readers for easy understanding of this rather complex branch of fiscal economics.

Author's Profile

M.M. Sury received his B.A. (Hons.), M.A., and Ph.D. degrees in economics from the University of Delhi. He taught economics in the same university for 42 years. Specialising in fiscal economics, he has published extensively on Indian fiscal system in recognised national and international journals, such as *Small Industry Bulletin for Asia and the Pacific* (United Nations, Bangkok), *Bulletin for International Fiscal Documentation* (International Fiscal Association, Amsterdam), *Asian-Pacific Tax and Investment Bulletin* (Singapore), *Journal of the Indian School of Political Economy* (Pune), *Indian Economic Journal* (Bombay), and *Margin* (New Delhi).

He was a Visiting Fellow at the International Bureau of Fiscal Documentation, Amsterdam (May 1989), a Fellow at the Indian Institute of Advanced Study, Shimla (1991-92) and a Visiting Fellow in the Department of Law and Management, University of Mauritius, Mauritius (September-October, 2000). He was Economic Adviser, First Delhi State Finance Commission (1996-97).

Contents

Preface

Black money and tax evasion are eating into the social and moral fabric of Indian society. They are undermining the socio-economic objectives of India's Five Year Plans. They are responsible for conspicuous and wasteful consumption, reduced savings, and increasing gap between the rich and the poor. Black money in social, economic and political space of the country has a debilitating effect on the institutions of governance and conduct of public policy in the country. Governance failure adversely affects the interests of vulnerable and disadvantaged sections of society. The success of an inclusive growth strategy critically hinges on the capacity of society to root out the evil of corruption and black money from its very foundations.

The effects of tax evasion, resulting in black money, on an economy are indeed disastrous. Tax evasion leads to the creation of black money which in turn is a menace to the economy in its own way. Tax evasion and black money encourage concentration of economic power in the hands of undesirable groups in the country.

Black money may be generated through the crude approach of not declaring or reporting the income or the activities leading to it. This is the likely approach in all cases of criminal, illegal, and impermissible activities. The same approach of not declaring or reporting activities and the income generated therefrom may also be followed in cases of failure to comply with regulatory obligations or tax evasion on income from legitimate activities. However, complete evasion or non-compliance may make such incomes vulnerable to detection by authorities and lead to adverse consequences for the generator.

As an alternative, a safer approach for generation of black money is often preferred, involving manipulation of financial records and accounting. Thus, the best way of classifying and understanding the various ways and means adopted by taxpayers for the generation of black money would be the *financial statement approach.* It elaborates different means by which the accounts prepared for reporting and presenting before the authorities are manipulated to misrepresent income, thereby generating income that amounts to black money.

With liberalisation of restrictions on cross-border flow of goods and services and relaxation of foreign exchange control, new opportunities have opened up for tax evasion through tax havens, misuse of transfer pricing, and other sophisticated methods. Globalisation has reduced the cost of these sophisticated methods thereby facilitating generation of black money and its transfer across the border. These changes require new strategies to curb black money. The fight against generation and accumulation of black money is far more complex and prolonged, requiring stronger intervention of the state. It needs a robust legal framework, commensurate administrative set up, and a very strong resolve to fight the menace.

A multi-pronged strategy is required to deal with the issue of generation of black money and its illicit transfer outside the country, and for bringing it back to India. The factors leading to generation of black money in India—along with the various measures attempted to counter it—make it clear that there is no single remedy to curb, control, and finally prevent the generation of black money. In fact, a comprehensive mix of well-defined strategies is needed by the Central and State Governments and put into practice by all their agencies in a co-ordinated manner.

New Delhi
June 2014

M.M. Sury

1

Black Money and Tax Evasion: Conceptual Settings

1.1 What is Black Money?

There is no uniform and universally acceptable definition of black money in fiscal literature. Generally speaking, the term *black money* stands for money earned by illegal means and kept secret and unaccounted for. It is widely used for smuggling activities, hoarding of scarce commodities (for the purpose of speculation, profiteering, and black marketing), bribing government officials, financing political activities, and ostentatious living. Secret business deals through black money in turn lead to tax evasion and a vicious circle is created in which one evil thrives on the other.

The term *black money* has many synonyms including *underground economy, parallel economy, shadow economy unofficial economy, and unaccounted economy.* All these terms usually refer to any income on which the taxes imposed by government or public authorities have not been paid. Thus, *black money* can be defined as assets or resources that have neither been reported to the public authorities at the time of their generation nor disclosed at any point of time during their possession.

In addition to wealth earned through illegal means, the term black money would also include legal income that is concealed from public authorities: (a) to evade payment of taxes (income tax, excise duty, sales tax, stamp duty etc), (b) to evade payment of other statutory contributions, and (c) to evade compliance with the provisions of industrial laws, and/or to evade compliance with other laws and administrative procedures.

Black money may be generated in two ways. Firstly, money may be generated through illegitimate activities not permissible under the law—like drug trade, terrorism, and corruption—and which are punishable under the legal framework of the state. Secondly, money may be generated and accumulated by failing to pay the dues to the public exchequer in one form or the other. In this case, the activities undertaken by the perpetrator could be legitimate and otherwise permissible under the law of the land but he fails to report the income so generated, comply with the tax requirements, or pay the dues to the public exchequer, leading to the generation of unaccounted wealth.

The comparison of the above two ways in which black money is generated is important to understand the problems and adopt appropriate policy measures to curb and control black money. It is clear that the first category is one where an iron fist is required on the part of government and its various law enforcing agencies. However, it is the second category where the issue becomes far more complex and may require new legislations/modification of existing laws and reforms in current policies and strategies to promote compliance with laws (particularly tax laws), regulations, and rules. The revamped institutional structure should also discourage the active economic agents of society from generating, hoarding, and illicitly transferring abroad such unaccounted wealth.

1.2 Sectors/Activities More Prone to Generation of Black Money and Tax Evasion

The source of generation of black money can lie in any sphere of economic activity. Nevertheless, there are certain sectors and activities which are more prone to black money generation. These include, *inter alia*, the following:

1. Land and real estate transactions.
2. Bullion and jewellery dealings.
3. Complex financial market transactions (derivatives).
4. Charitable (non-profit) activities.
5. Informal sector and cash economy.
6. Self-employed professionals.

7. External trade and transfer pricing.

1.2.1 Land and Real Estate Transactions: Due to rising prices of real estate, the high tax incidence applicable on real estate transactions—in the form of stamp duty [1] and capital gains tax—can create incentives for tax evasion through under-reporting of transaction price. This can lead to both generation and investment of black money. The buyer has the option of investing his black money by paying cash in addition to the documented sale consideration. This also leads to generation of black money in the hands of the recipient.

1.2.2 Bullion and Jewellery Dealings: Cash sales in the gold and jewellery trade are quite common and serve two purposes. The purchase allows the buyer the option of converting black money into gold and bullion, while it gives the trader the option of keeping his unaccounted wealth in the form of stock, not disclosed in the books or valued at less than market price.

1.2.3 Complex Financial Market Transactions: Financial market transactions can involve black money in different forms. Rigging of markets by the market operators is one such means. This may involve use of dummy companies, trading in derivatives [2], participatory notes (PNs) [3] and other forms of manipulated trading.

1.2.4 Charitable (Non-profit) Activities: Taxation laws allow certain privileges and incentives for promoting charitable (non-profit) activities. Misuse of such benefits and manipulations through entities claimed to be constituted for non-profit motive are among possible sources of generation of black money.

Generally, charitable trusts are not required to pay tax on donations received by them. Similarly, income tax laws allow charitable contributions as deductions from taxable income. Since marginal rates of tax are high at upper brackets of income, charitable contributions are less costly to wealthy people.

These provisions are sometimes misused in the sense that donors exercise considerable control in managing the affairs of trusts/institutions to which charitable contributions are made. Private or family interest in the management of charitable trusts leads to control in the use of what are essentially public funds. Family control over a charitable trust generally leads to promoting private interest, defeating in the process the essential purpose of the tax concession. To quote, "Charitable organisations, non-government organisations (NGOs), and associations receiving foreign contributions are required to file an annual return to the Ministry of Home Affairs in Form FC-3. In the said form, only the name and address of the foreign donors are mentioned, with no further details of the beneficial owners. It is possible that in many such cases, the black money generated by Indians is being routed back to India". [4]

1.2.5 Informal Sector and Cash Economy: In its Report on Definitional and Statistical Issues Relating to the Informal Economy, submitted in 2008, the National Commission for Enterprises in the Unorganized Sector (Chairman: Arjun Sengupta), defined unorganized (informal) sector as the "sector consisting of all unincorporated private enterprises owned by individuals or households engaged in the sale and production of goods and services operated on a proprietary or partnership basis and with less than ten total workers". [5]

The issue of black money is related to the magnitude of cash transactions in the informal economy. Factors like dependence on agriculture, existence of a large informal sector, and insufficient banking infrastructure with large un-banked and under-banked areas contribute to the large cash economy in India.

1.2.6 Self-employed Professionals: Although evasion of tax is a common tendency among people belonging to different groups, opportunities for it vary according to the nature of income earned by taxpayers. In the case of income from salaries and interest from deposits, evasion is less likely because of proper recording and auditing of transactions, and deduction of tax at source. However, opportunities for tax evasion are very large in the case of self-employed in business and professions. Doctors, lawyers, architects, property dealers, individual contractors, jewellers, caterers, event managers can evade taxes more easily than others. They can insist on their customers to pay them in cash or accept invoices which underestimate the payment.

Moreover, salaried persons envy tax evasion opportunities available to self-employed professionals and retail traders, and are tempted to conceal their incomes from non-salary sources.

1.2.7 External Trade and Transfer Pricing: Differing tax rates in different countries can create perverse incentives for corporations to shift taxable income from jurisdictions with relatively high tax rates to jurisdictions with relatively low tax rates as a means of minimising their tax liability. For example, a foreign parent company could use internal *transfer prices* for reducing its worldwide tax payment. In fact, transfer pricing [6] has emerged as the biggest tool for generation and transfer of black money.

1.3 Tax Evasion: Meaning

Tax evasion exists in all countries, though in varying degrees. It is a serious problem in developing countries which are in the process of evolving their tax systems.

Tax evasion is an illegal attempt to reduce the tax payable by deliberately under-reporting or not reporting taxable incomes or concealing one's true *state of affairs* from tax authorities. Tax evasion is a criminal offence and if detected is punishable by financial penalties or even by imprisonment or both.

1.3.1 Tax Evasion and Tax Avoidance: Tax avoidance means preventing or reducing one's tax liability through manipulations within the framework of existing tax legislation. Tax avoidance, as against tax evasion, is legally permissible and hence a legitimate aim of taxpayers.

Tax avoidance is resorted to through such devices as formation of holding companies to claim artificial deductions, constitution of trusts and family partnerships, transfer of income earning assets to one's wife and children for fractioning income for tax purposes, investing in provident funds and life insurance policies, and manipulation of capital gains.

Since tax avoidance has a colour of legality about it, clever taxpayers do their best to avoid or keep down tax payments. This may force the government to raise tax rates, making the less clever assessees bear a disproportionate tax burden.

Tax laws in many countries incorporate anti-tax avoidance provisions under which certain incomes are included in an assessee's total income, though such incomes legally belong to other persons. For example, in India, Sections 60 to 65 of the Income Tax Act, 1961, deal with instances where an assessee may attempt to reduce his tax liability either by transferring his assets in favour of his family members or by arranging his sources of income in such a manner that tax incidence falls on others, whereas benefit of income, directly or indirectly, is derived by the assessee himself. Thus, income arising to the spouse, minor child, son's wife, son's minor child and certain other persons are clubbed with the assessee's income in certain circumstances. In this regard, the Indian income tax law deviates from the general principle that a person can be assessed in respect of his own income.

1.4 International Tax Avoidance and Evasion

While it is true that international business operations are exposed to the risk of being subject to double taxation, it cannot be gainsaid that such activities provide opportunities for tax avoidance/evasion. Following are the devices generally applied for the purpose.

1.4.1 Transfer Pricing: It refers to the price attached to transactions between the divisions (e.g. branches or subsidiaries) of a company. Transfer pricing is usually considered in a global context, particularly in relation to cross-frontier transactions within a multinational company.

Determination of transfer price has significance in relation to such matters as taxation, exchange restrictions, and currency fluctuations. The incentive for transfer price manipulations is provided by varying rates of taxation in countries where a multinational company operates. Thus, where goods are being transferred from a company in a low tax country to a subsidiary company in a high tax country, there is a clear tax incentive if a high transfer price is ensured to maximise profit within the low tax country.

Similarly, sales of a multinational group may be routed through a specially formed tax haven distribution company. The tax haven company purchases goods from affiliated companies at the lowest possible prices and sells to independent purchasers at the full market price, ensuring that most or all of the profit from the transaction is earned in the tax haven.

Due to the inherent difficulties in determining a fair or market price for inter-company transactions, a multinational company has always the option to fix artificial transfer prices.

A. Arm's Length Price: It refers to market price that would have been negotiated by unrelated parties engaged in the same or similar transactions under the same or similar conditions. Arm's length standard is used to prevent the use of transfer pricing technique for tax avoidance. Many countries exercise their right to adjust reported transfer prices to conform to an arm's length criterion. Implementing the arm's length principle is a difficult task for tax authorities.

1.4.2 Tax Treaty Shopping: It is a situation where a person resident in a third country seeks to obtain benefits of a double tax treaty between two other countries. A double tax treaty confers substantial benefits on the residents of treaty countries. Let us suppose that Mr. Wilson, resident in country A, wants to invest in country B. Assuming that there is no double tax treaty between country A and country B, any income received by Mr. Wilson will be subject to full rates of taxation in country B. In such a situation, Mr. Wilson may find it advantageous to channel his investment to country B through a company in country C because country C has double tax treaties with countries A and B. For example, Mauritius is a popular treaty shopping haven for many foreign companies for channelling investments into India because of favourable tax treaty provisions. [7]

To prevent the misuse of tax treaties through tax treaty shopping, many countries take care to include anti-treaty abuse provisions in these agreements. For example, there is a specific clause in the double tax treaty between India and USA under which benefits of the treaty are available only to genuine residents of either country. In other words, the treaty restricts the use of USA as a treaty shopping centre for investments in India.

1.5 Global Concerns against Black Money/Tax Evasion

The global economic conditions deteriorated sharply during the year 2008 with several advanced economies experiencing their sharpest declines in the post-Second World War period. The associated adverse shocks spreading across developing countries accentuated the synchronised global slowdown. The global financial environment entered a crisis phase following the growing distress among large international financial institutions and the declaration of bankruptcy of Lehman Brothers.

The financial crisis of 2008 and the resultant need for protecting revenues further strengthened the need for coordinated global efforts to tackle the challenges posed by tax haven-mediated arrangements for evading tax.

1.5.1 United Nations Convention against Illicit Traffic in Narcotic Drugs and Psychotropic Substances: The purpose of this Convention is to promote cooperation among the parties so that they may more effectively address the various aspects of illicit traffic in narcotic drugs and psychotropic substances having an international dimension. The Convention also calls for criminalisation of money laundering, the freezing, seizure and confiscation of the proceeds of crime, and international cooperation. India joined this Convention on March 27, 1990.

1.5.2 Multilateral Convention on Mutual Administrative Assistance in Tax Matters: This Convention was developed jointly by the Council of Europe and the Organization for

Economic Development and Co-operation (OECD) [8] and was opened for signature by the member states of both organizations on January 25, 1998. This multilateral instrument, which was initially signed by 15 countries, provides for all possible forms of administrative cooperation between states in the assessment and collection of taxes, in particular with a view to combating tax avoidance and evasion.

In response to the April 2009 call by the G20 [9] for a global instrument to fight international tax evasion and avoidance, the Convention has been brought up to the internationally agreed standard on information exchange for tax purposes, in particular by requiring the exchange of bank information on request through an amending Protocol, which entered into force on June 1, 2011. The amended Protocol also provides for the opening of the Convention to all countries. India signed the Convention on January 26, 2012 and ratified it on February 2, 2012, thus becoming the first country outside the OECD and European countries to join it. There are at present 33 signatories to the Convention and 13 of them have ratified it.

This Convention provides many advantages. As more countries sign it, the task of information exchange will get increasingly facilitated. It is likely to be an important instrument for cooperation in the area of assistance in tax collection. A unique feature of this convention is the facility for serving of notices issued by one tax administration through another tax administration.

1.5.3 United Nations Convention against Corruption: On May 9, 2011, India became the 152nd country to ratify this Convention which was signed on December 9, 2005. The objectives of this Convention are as under:

1. To promote and strengthen measures for preventing and combating corruption more efficiently and effectively.
2. To promote, facilitate, and support international cooperation and technical assistance in the prevention of and fight against corruption including in asset recovery.

3. To promote integrity, accountability measures, and the criminalisation of the most prevalent forms of corruption in both public and private sectors.

The Convention requires the state parties to criminalise bribery of national public officials, foreign public officials and officials of public international organizations, embezzlement, misappropriation or other divisions of property by a public official, laundering of proceeds of crime, obstruction of justice, and illicit enrichment.

Under the Convention, countries should have mechanisms for freezing, seizure, and confiscation of the proceeds of crime and cooperate in criminal matters by extradition and mutual legal assistance to the greatest possible extent. The return of assets is a fundamental objective of this Convention and countries are to afford one another the widest measure of cooperation and assistance in this regard. It prescribes mechanisms for recovery of property through international cooperation for purposes of confiscation.

1.5.4 United Nations Convention against Transnational Organized Crime (Palermo Convention): On May 5, 2011, India ratified this Convention which was signed on December 12, 2002. The purpose of this Convention is to promote international cooperation in preventing and combating transnational organized crime more effectively. Under the Convention, countries are to take measures against smuggling of migrants by land, sea, and air as well as manufacturing and trafficking of firearms and ammunition. The Convention will help India get international cooperation in tracing, seizure, freezing, and confiscation of the proceeds of crimes under a wide range of mutual legal assistance clauses, even with countries with which it has no mutual legal assistance treaties.

1.5.5 International Convention for the Suppression of the Financing of Terrorism: India signed this Convention on September 8, 2000 and ratified it on April 22, 2003. It requires each state party to take appropriate measures, in accordance with its domestic legal principles, for the detection and freezing, seizure, or forfeiture of any funds used or allocated for the purposes of committing the offences described, as well as take alleged offenders into custody, prosecute or extradite them, cooperate in preventive measures and countermeasures, and exchange information and evidence needed in related criminal proceedings. The offences referred to in the Convention are deemed to be extraditable offences between state parties under existing extradition treaties and under the Convention itself.

1.5.6 Financial Action Task Force (FATF): It is an inter-governmental body established in 1989 by the Ministers of its Member jurisdictions. The objectives of the FATF are to set standards and promote effective implementation of legal, regulatory and operational measures for combating money laundering, terrorist financing and other related threats to the integrity of the international financial system. The FATF is therefore a *policy-making body* which works to generate the necessary political will to bring about national legislative and regulatory reforms in these areas.

The FATF has developed a series of Recommendations that are recognised as the international standard for combating of money laundering and the financing of terrorism and proliferation of weapons of mass destruction. They form the basis for a co-ordinated response to these threats to the integrity of the financial system and help ensure a level playing field. First issued in 1990, the FATF Recommendations were revised in 1996, 2001, 2003 and most recently in 2012 to ensure that they remain up to date and relevant, and they are intended to be of universal application.

The FATF monitors the progress of its members in implementing necessary measures, reviews money laundering and terrorist financing techniques and counter-measures, and promotes the adoption and implementation of appropriate measures globally. In collaboration with other international stakeholders, the FATF works to identify national-level vulnerabilities with the aim of protecting the international financial system from misuse.

The FATF's decision making body, the FATF Plenary, meets three times per year.

1.5.7 Asia/Pacific Group on Money Laundering (APG): It is an international organisation (regionally focused) consisting of 41 members and a number of international and regional observers including the United Nations, IMF, FATF, Asian Development Bank, ASEAN Secretariat, Pacific Islands Forum Secretariat and World Bank.

APG is closely affiliated with the Financial Action Task Force (FATF), whose Secretariat is located in the OECD headquarters in Paris, France. All APG members commit to effectively implement the FATF's international standards for anti-money laundering, combating the financing of terrorism and the financing of proliferation, referred to as the 40 Recommendations. The 40 Recommendations were revised and adopted by the FATF membership after world-wide consultation (including the private sector) in February 2012. Part of this commitment includes implementing targeted financial sanctions against terrorism and the financing of the proliferation of weapons of mass destruction (WMD).

End Notes

1. Under entry 63 of List II (State List) in the Seventh Schedule of the Constitution of India, stamp duty is levied by the State Governments on the registration of property or other conveyances. Till recently, the stamp duty rates were quite high in most states and the procedures for evaluating the conveyances were also complicated. In this context, the Tenth Five Year Plan (2002-07) remarked, "Stamp duty needs to be paid on all documents which are registered and the rate varies from state to state. With stamp duty rates of 13 percent in Delhi, 14.5 percent in Uttar Pradesh and 12.5 percent in Haryana, India has perhaps one of the highest levels of stamp duty. Some states even have double stamp incidence, first on land and then on its development. In contrast the maximum rate levied in most developed markets whether in Singapore or Europe is in the range of 1-2 percent. Even the National Housing and Habitat Policy, 1998, recommended a stamp duty rate of 2-3 percent.

Most of the methods to avoid registration are basically to avoid payment of high stamp duty.

Another fall out of high stamp duty rates is the understatement of the proceeds of a sale. This is also linked to payment of income tax and capital gains tax. When registration has not been effected, a transfer is not deemed to have taken place and hence capital gains tax can be totally avoided. Thus, the present provisions in various laws and their poor implementation have led to a situation where there is considerable financial loss to the exchequer on account of understatement of sale proceeds, non-registration and consequent non-payment of stamp duty and avoidance of capital gains tax." [Government of India, Planning Commission, *Tenth Five Year Plan* (2002-07), Volume II, pp. 833-834.]

Of late, states have undertaken reforms by reducing the duty rates and streamlining procedures for evaluation of property. After the reduction of rates, the general experience has been revenue-augmentation due to improved compliance of law.

2. For meaning of financial derivatives, see end note 2 of chapter 3 of this book.
3. For meaning of participatory note (PN), see section 3.6 of chapter 3 of this book.
4. Government of India, Ministry of Finance, *White Paper on Black Money,* May 2012, para 2.8.5.
5. National Commission for Enterprises in the Unorganized Sector [NCEUS] (Chairman: Arjun Sengupta), was set up by the Government of India on September 20, 2004, to "review the status of unorganized/informal sector in India including the nature of enterprises, their size, spread and scope, and magnitude of employment," This step was taken to ensure the welfare and well-being of all workers, particularly those in the unorganized sector, who constitute more than 93 percent of workforce. NCEUS prepared and submitted to the Government a number of reports before submitting its final report in 2009.
6. For meaning of transfer pricing, see section 1.4.1 of this chapter.
7. For Issues relating to Indo-Mauritius tax treaty, see section 7.8 of chapter 7 of this book.
8. OECD is an international organisation of industrialised nations with the following two-fold objectives: (i) To contribute through co-operative efforts to economic growth, employment, financial

stability and rising standard of living in member countries. (ii) To promote economic development of all nations and trade among them by assisting countries in their efforts to achieve these goals. Based in Paris, OECD was formed on December 14, 1960 as a successor organisation to the Organisation for European Economic Co-operation (OEEC), whose main purpose was to co-ordinate the post-World War II economic recovery of Europe and to administer aid provided by USA through the Marshall Plan.

9. The Group of Twenty (G-20) Finance Ministers and Central Bank Governors was established in 1999 to bring together systemically important industrialized and developing economies to discuss key issues in the global economy. The inaugural meeting of the G-20 took place in Berlin, on December 15-16, 1999, hosted by German and Canadian finance ministers.

   The G-20 is an informal forum that promotes open and constructive discussion between industrial and emerging-market countries on key issues related to global economic stability. By contributing to the strengthening of the international financial architecture and providing opportunities for dialogue on national policies, international co-operation, and international financial institutions, the G-20 helps to support growth and development across the globe.

   The G-20 was created as a response both to the financial crises of the late 1990s and to a growing recognition that key emerging-market countries were not adequately included in the core of global economic discussion and governance.

   The G-20 is made up of the finance ministers and central bank governors of 19 countries: Argentina, Australia, Brazil, Canada, China, France, Germany, India, Indonesia, Italy, Japan, Mexico, Russia, Saudi Arabia, South Africa, South Korea, Turkey, United Kingdom, United States of America. The European Union is the 20th member of the G-20.

2

Causes and Consequences of Black Money and Tax Evasion

2.1 Generation of Black Money: Leading Factors

2.1.1 Generation of Black Money through Illegal Activities: The *criminal component* of black money includes a host of illegal activities. Such activities—anti-social in nature—include, *inter alia*, the following:

1. Smuggling of goods.
2. Forgery, embezzlement, counterfeit currency, and other financial frauds (chit funds etc.).
3. Production/trade of contraband goods (e.g. narcotics, illicit liquor and arms).
4. Illegal mining and illegal felling of forests.
5. Hoarding and black marketing of price-controlled goods and services.
6. Theft, robbery, kidnapping and extortion, human trafficking, sexual exploitation and blackmailing.
7. Bribes to those holding public offices to secure favours: (a) altering land use, (b) regularizing authorized constructions, (c) speed money to circumvent/fast track procedures, and (d) commission to secure government purchase orders.

All above-mentioned activities are illegal and reflect declining social and moral values. These illegal activities are punishable under various Acts of the Central and State Governments which are administered by various law enforcement agencies. Effective implementation of these Acts is the responsibility of both the Central and State Governments. Some of these offences are included in the schedule of the Prevention of Money Laundering Act, 2002.

2.1.2 Generation of Black Money through Legal Activities: Significant amount of black money, however, is generated through legally permissible economic activities. Though lawful, such activities are not disclosed/reported to the public authorities as per provisions of the law, thereby converting such income into black money. The failure to report/disclose such activities/income may be with the objective of evading taxes or avoiding the cost of compliance related to such reporting/disclosure under some other law.

Generally, a high burden of taxation provides a strong temptation to evade taxes. Sometimes the procedural regulations can be such that complying with them may increase the probability of further scrutiny and thereby the incidence of the burden of compliance. Such situations create incentive to conceal one's true state of affairs and thereby remain outside the reported and accounted proportion of one's activities.

With increased globalisation [1] and economic liberalisation, there has been a manifold increase in cross-border transactions. This has also resulted in increased opportunities for sophisticated devices to avoid tax payment using the different tax rules of different countries and use of tax havens. Global trade amongst various arms of multinational companies (MNCs) has also increased substantially and accounts for a significant proportion of global trade. It also means increasing misuse of transfer pricing, leading to estimations that developing countries might be losing significant resources due to transfer pricing manipulation.

One of the difficulties in preventing abuse of such transfer pricing arrangements is the large disparity between resources deployed by these multinationals and those available with tax administrators, particularly of developing countries. This requires enormous reforms for improving the capacity of tax administration and equipping it with the necessary resources to deal with such modern challenges.

2.2 Causes of Tax Evasion

2.2.1 High Level of Tax Rates: Among the host of causes of tax evasion and hence the generation of black money, the level of tax rates is probably the most crucial. It is widely believed that higher the rate of tax, the greater is the tendency to evade taxes. High tax rates make tax evasion more tempting. Tax evaders readily take greater risks if they know that in the event of success the reward is high. Per contra, it can be expected that low tax rates improve tax compliance and broaden the tax base.

2.2.2 Less Respect for Government and its Laws: Tax evasion is more in countries where there is general apathy on the part of people towards the government and its laws. People will have less respect for tax laws if they perceive the tax system to be unfair in terms of level of taxation (tax-GDP ratio) [2] and/or distribution of tax burden among various classes (i.e. tax equity). [3] Similarly, there can be a feeling among taxpayers that government is indulging in wasteful expenditure (e.g. digging the roads too often), spending excessively on government functionaries, permitting loan waivers, maintaining perpetually sick public undertakings, and granting unnecessary subsidies. Tax evasion by politicians sends wrong signals to the general public that non-compliance is acceptable.

It is necessary to change the attitude of the people towards Government and its laws. In this connection, the Indian Tax Reforms Committee, 1991, observed, "...there is a widespread feeling among the electorate that there is considerable waste in government expenditure, that there is excess staff and that the tail to teeth ratio is unduly high. And with it all, it is generally felt that the public which pays the taxes gets poor service and members of the public are treated often not as masters who pay but as supplicants". [4]

2.2.3 Lenient Penal Action: Lenient penal action in case violation of law is detected also encourages tax evasion. In general, countries with relatively poor implementation of regulations tend to have a higher share of unaccounted economy, whereas countries with properly implemented regulations and sound deterrence have smaller *black* economies.

2.2.4 Nature of the Economy: The problem of tax evasion in underdeveloped countries is associated with the peculiar characteristics of their economies which, in most cases, are agriculture-based in the sense that a substantial part of national income originates from and the majority of the work force is engaged in agriculture. Moreover, there is widespread illiteracy, lack of accounting practices, limited monetisation and shortage of administrative resources in these countries. A regime of controls, licences, and shortages also breeds tax evasion and black money.

2.3 Consequences of Black Money/Tax Evasion

The nexus between tax evasion and black money and its distortion of the redistributive role of tax policy was noted by India's Seventh Five Year Plan as follows, "With a sizeable proportion of income and wealth evading taxation, the redistributive impact of progressive taxation had been severely blunted. A reduction in the scale of black income generation would improve distribution of income and wealth after taxation. Besides, if the magnitude of tax evasion is significantly reduced, there would be a greater volume of tax revenue, and a greater volume of public expenditure benefiting the poorer section of the population would become possible". [5]

Black money in social, economic and political space of the country has a debilitating effect on the institutions of governance and conduct of public policy in the country. Governance failure adversely affects the interests of vulnerable and disadvantaged sections of society. The success of an inclusive growth strategy [6] critically depends on the capacity of society to root out the evil of corruption and black money from its very foundations. Undoubtedly, India needs a speedy transition towards a more transparent and result-oriented economic system.

The effects of tax evasion, resulting in black money, on an economy are indeed disastrous. Some of these are listed below:

1. Tax evasion cuts at the very root of the revenue potential

of a tax system and therefore hinders the resource mobilisation efforts of a government. Lack of funds may distort implementation of development plans and force a government to resort to deficit financing in case public expenditure is inelastic.

2. Tax evasion may interfere with the declared economic policies of a government by distorting saving/investment patterns and availability of resources for various sectors of the economy. For instance, government may impose credit restrictions to discourage certain activities (e.g. speculation) but money saved through tax evasion may finance and encourage the same activities.
3. Evasion of tax seriously undermines the equity attribute of a tax system. Honest taxpayers, who are obliged to bear disproportionate tax burden, feel demoralised and tempted to join the tax evaders' camp.
4. Tax evasion leads to the creation of black money which in turn is a menace to the economy in its own way. Tax evasion and black money encourage concentration of economic power in the hands of undesirable groups in the country.
5. Tax evasion eats into the time and energy of tax administration which is obliged to unravel the intricate manipulations of tax dodgers.
6. Tax evasion leads to degradation of social and moral standards. Social abuses like bribery, intimidation, blackmailing, tampering with official records, submitting fake documents etc. all go with tax evasion.

To conclude, with liberalisation of restrictions on cross-border flow of goods and services and relaxation of foreign exchange control, new opportunities have opened up for tax evasion through tax havens, misuse of transfer pricing, and other sophisticated methods. Globalisation has reduced the cost of these sophisticated methods thereby facilitating generation of black money and its transfer across the border. These changes require new strategies to curb black money.

The fight against generation and accumulation of black money is far more complex and prolonged, requiring stronger intervention of the state. It needs a robust legal framework, commensurate administrative set up, and a very strong resolve to fight the menace.

End Notes

1. Globalisation implies widening and deepening integration with the *globe*, i.e. with people and processes abroad. The trend towards the evolution of a global society is generally thought of in economic terms and in terms of the consequences of the revolution in communication technologies. There is undoubtedly much greater economic integration among the nations of the world today. Globalisation is widely seen as the most important factor that could influence economies of nations the world over in the new millennium. The rapid advancement in information technology and communications has made it not just possible but absolutely essential for economies of the world to adapt or fall by the wayside.
2. Level of taxation in a country is traditionally judged in terms of the ratio which taxes bear to some measure of national income. This ratio is called tax-GDP ratio and the change in it is determined by variations in both the numerator (total tax revenue) and the denominator (national income).
3. Tax equity refers to *fair* or *just* or *equitable* distribution of tax burden among taxpayers. Though fairness and justness in taxation are universally accepted, these terms are rarely defined rigorously and can be interpreted in various ways. Hence, there is no unanimity of opinion as to the type of tax system which results in the most equitable distribution of tax burden.

   There are two main approaches to tax equity in tax literature: the Benefit Principle of Taxation which states that tax payments should be proportional to the benefits derived from government services, and the Ability-to-Pay Principle of Taxation which holds that each taxpayer should contribute to the public exchequer in line with his ability-to-pay.
4. Government of India, Ministry of Finance, *Interim Report of the Tax Reforms Committee* (Chairman: Raja Chelliah), December 1991, p. 44.

5. Government of India, Planning Commission, *The Seventh Five Year Plan, 1985-90*, Vol. I, p. 71.
6. Inclusive growth may be defined as growth that promotes equal opportunities and increases access to these opportunities, i.e. growth that allows all members of society to participate in and contribute equally to development efforts, regardless of individual circumstances. This concept appears in Asian Development Bank's (ADB) *Strategy 2020* that examines the extent of inequality of opportunities and to what extent it can be overcome by different types of growth process. The main idea in the ADB's approach is to focus on productive employment as an important element of inclusive growth.

   Inclusive growth, defined in a broader sense has three dimensions: (i) Equity among all sections of the society; (ii) Equity among all sectors of the economy; and (iii) Equity among all regions in the country.

   Thus, inclusive growth means inter-group, inter-sector as well as inter-regional equity. Growth is inclusive when it creates economic opportunities along with ensuring equal access to them.

3

Methods to Generate Black Money and Evade Taxes

3.1 Cobwebs of Black Money Generation

Black money may be generated through the crude approach of not declaring or reporting the income or the activities leading to it. This is the likely approach in all cases of criminal, illegal, and impermissible activities. The same approach of not declaring or reporting activities and the income generated therefrom may also be followed in cases of failure to comply with regulatory obligations or tax evasion on income from legitimate activities. However, complete evasion or non-compliance may make such incomes vulnerable to detection by authorities and lead to adverse consequences for the generator.

As an alternative, a safer approach for generation of black money is often preferred, involving manipulation of financial records and accounting. Thus, the best way of classifying and understanding the various ways and means adopted by taxpayers for the generation of black money would be the *financial statement approach*. It elaborates different means by which the accounts prepared for reporting and presenting before the authorities are manipulated to misrepresent income, thereby generating income that amounts to black money.

As is well-known, any transaction entered into by the taxpayer must be reported in books of account which are summarized at the end of the year in the form of financial statements. The financial statements basically comprise: (a) statement of income and expenditure called *profit and loss account* or *income and expenditure account*, and (b) statement of assets and liabilities called *balance sheet*.

Different kinds of manipulations of financial statements

resulting in tax evasion and the generation of black money are elaborated in the following paragraphs.

3.2 Out of Book Transactions

3.2.1 No Books of Account: This is one of the simplest and most widely adopted methods of tax evasion and generation of black money. Transactions that may result in taxation of receipts or income are not entered in the books of account by the taxpayer. The taxpayer either does not maintain books of account or maintains two sets or records partial receipts only. This mode is generally prevalent among the micro and small enterprises and providers of unskilled and semi-skilled services.

3.2.2 Parallel Books of Accounts: This is a practice usually adopted by those who are obliged under the law, or due to business needs, to maintain books of account. In order to evade reporting activities or the income generated from them, they may resort to maintaining two sets of books of account—one for their own consumption with the objective of managing their business and the other one for the regulatory and tax authorities (income tax, excise, VAT). The second set of books of account, which is maintained for the purpose of satisfying the legal and regulatory obligations of reporting to different authorities, may be manipulated by omitting receipts or falsely inflating expenses, for the purpose of evading taxes or other regulatory requirements.

Other methods under this category include: (a) unaccounted assets, and (b) investments in shares of listed companies through dummy entities.

3.3 Manipulation of Books of Account

When books of accounts are required to be maintained by taxpayers under different laws (e.g. Income Tax Act, 1961; Companies Act, 1956) it may become difficult for these taxpayers to indulge in out of book transactions or to maintain parallel books of accounts. Such parties may resort to manipulation of the books of accounts to evade taxes.

3.3.1 Manipulation of Sales/Receipts: A taxpayer is required to pay taxes on profit or income which is the difference between sale proceeds or receipts and expenditure. Thus, manipulation of sales or receipts is the easiest method of tax evasion. Other innovative devices may include diversion of sales to associated enterprises, which may become more important if such enterprises are located in different tax jurisdictions and thereby may also give rise to issues related to international taxation and transfer pricing.

In the case of dummy associate entity, there can be a plethora of possible arrangements entered into by such entities to aid generation of black money. In its simplest form, the associate entity may not report its activities or income at all. The main entity may show sales to such a dummy associate entity at a lower price, thereby reducing its reported profits.

More complex scenarios can emerge if the dummy associate entity is situated in a low tax jurisdiction having very low tax rates. Thus, the profit of the Indian entity will be transferred to the low tax jurisdiction and money will be accumulated by the taxpayer in the books of accounts of the entity in the low tax jurisdiction.

Under-reporting of production is another means of artificially reducing tax liability. It may be resorted to for the purpose of evading central excise, sales tax, or income tax.

In short, the following means can be applied to manipulate sales/receipts: (a) suppression of sales/receipts, (b) diversion of sales to associated enterprises (dummy or genuine), (c) inter-relation between unaccounted sales and purchases, (d) artificial deferment of revenues, and (e) stamping of incorrect price.

3.3.2 Manipulation of Expenses: Since the income on which taxes are payable is arrived at after deducting the expenses of the business from the receipts, manipulation of expenses is a commonly adopted method of tax evasion. The expenses may be manipulated under different heads and result in under-reporting of income. It may involve inflation of expenses, sometimes by obtaining bogus or inflated invoices from the so called *bill masters*, who make bogus vouchers and charge nominal commission for this facility. Sometimes it can also involve *hawala* operators, who operate shell entities in the form of proprietorship firms, partnership firms, companies, and trusts. These operators may accept cheques for payments claimed as expense and return cash after charging some commission.

There have been instances of claims of bogus expenses to foreign entities. The payments can be shown to foreign entities in the form of advertisement and marketing expenses or commission for purchases or sales. The funds may be remitted to the account of the foreign taxpayer and the money can either be withdrawn in cash or remitted back to India in the form of non-taxable receipts. Such money may also be accumulated in the form of unaccounted assets of the Indian taxpayer abroad.

Besides inflation of purchase/raw material cost, expenses like labour charges, entertainment expenses, and commission can be inflated or falsely booked to reduce profits.

3.3.3 Manipulation of Capital: The balance sheet of the taxpayer contains details of assets, liabilities, and capital. The capital of the taxpayer is the accumulated wealth which is invested in the form of assets or as working capital of the business. Manipulation of capital can be one of the ways of laundering black money and introducing it in the books of accounts. Manipulation of capital can take place, *inter alia*, through following means: (a) shares at high premium, (b) bogus gifts, and (c) bogus capital gains and purchase of bogus losses.

3.3.4 Manipulation of Closing Stock: Suppression of closing stock both in terms of quality and value is one of the most common methods of understating profit. Refiner versions of such practice may include omission of goods in transit paid for and debited to purchases, or omission of goods sent to the customer for approval. A more common approach is undervaluation of inventory (stock of unsold goods), which means that while the expenses are being accounted for in the books, the value being added is not accounted for, thereby artificially reducing the profits.

3.3.5 Manipulation of Capital Expenses: Over-invoicing plant and equipment or any capital asset is an approach adopted to claim higher depreciation and thereby reduce the profit of the business. Increase in capital can also be a means of enabling the businessman to borrow more funds from banks or raise capital from the market. It has been seen that such measures are sometimes resorted to at the time of bringing out a capital issue.

3.3.6 International Transactions through Associate Enterprises: Another way of manipulating accounted profits and taxes payable thereon may involve using associated enterprises in low tax jurisdictions through which goods or other material may be passed on to the concern. Inter-corporate transactions between these associate enterprises belonging to the same group or owned and controlled by the same set of parties may be arranged and manipulated in a way that leads to evasion of taxes. This can often be achieved by arrangements that shift taxable income to the low tax jurisdictions or tax havens, and may lead to accumulation of black money earned from within India to another country.

3.4 Devices Adopted to Evade Taxes

3.4.1 Income Tax: Income tax is evaded through non-reporting, under-reporting and misreporting of income (e.g. showing non-agricultural income as agricultural income). [1]

The following devices are generally employed to evade income tax:

1. Non-reporting/under-reporting of taxable income.
2. Maintaining multiple set of account books, fraudulent changes in account books, and keeping transactions out of account books.
3. Opening and operating bank accounts under assumed names.

4. Doing business in the name of dummies.
5. Over-reporting expenses.
6. Fragmenting income to reduce tax liability.
7. Under-invoicing sales and other transfer pricing manipulations.

3.4.2 Excise Duties: Excise evasion is generally resorted to by adopting, *inter alia*, following malpractices.

1. Incorrect accountal of goods.
2. Undervaluation of goods.
3. Flouting the conditions subject to which any goods may be exempted from duty.

3.4.3 Value-Added Tax (VAT): The proponents of VAT claim that evasion under it is difficult and minimal. The tax credit method ensures cross-checking of the records of taxpayers through invoices. Buyer firms insist on supplier firms to furnish invoices which help the former to claim tax credit. Since tax liability of a single taxpayer under VAT is only a fraction of the total amount of tax, the incentive for evasion is relatively weak. Even a successful evasion would mean less revenue loss as compared to the one suffered under a system of turnover tax on gross value (excise duty or sales tax).

Despite the self-policing nature of VAT, opportunities do exist under it for evasion and fraud. In fact, VAT provides opportunities for fraud (fictitious claims for refunds) which are not available under other forms of commodity taxation. The methods commonly applied to defraud tax authorities under VAT include, *inter alia,* the following.

1. Use of fake invoices to claim tax credit.
2. Tax credit claims on purchases for personal use.
3. Over-reporting of sales of zero-rated goods.
4. Secret deals between buyers and sellers as regards issuance of receipts.
5. Formation of fake companies which sell receipts to traders to enable them to claim tax credit on inputs.

Thus, VAT is as susceptible to evasion and fraud as any other tax. An efficient tax machinery capable of cross-checking a large number of invoices through an elaborate computer system is a pre-requisite for the successful implementation of VAT.

3.4.4 Customs Duties: Evasion of customs duties takes place through following malpractices.

1. Invoice misclassification.
2. Manipulation of documents.
3. Suppression of quantities imported.

3.5 Tax Havens

The term *tax haven* has been widely used since the 1950s. However, there is no precise definition of the term. The expression is used to describe any country or locality which levies very low taxes, or none at all, on foreigners. Tax havens can be broadly classified into three categories based on the degree of tax concessions.

1. Where there is no tax at all, e.g. Bahamas, Bermuda, and Cayman Islands.
2. Where only a low rate of tax is imposed, e.g. British Virgin Islands, Hong Kong, and Isle of Man.
3. Where the tax system favours particular activities or entities, e.g. Luxembourg, Panama, and Switzerland.

Tax havens are used in a number of ways to avoid/evade high taxes of non-tax haven countries. The commonest device is to use a tax haven only as a conduit for transactions the real economic impact of which is located elsewhere. Thus, international transactions between two high tax rate countries may be channelled through a tax haven company so that any resulting profit is realised in the tax haven with a consequent minimisation of tax.

The Organization for Economic Co-operation and Development (OECD) initially defined tax havens as being characterised by no or very low taxes, lack of effective exchange of information, and lack of transparency about substantial activities. It listed 35 countries/jurisdictions as tax havens in the year 2000.

3.5.1 Offshore Financial Centres: Some of the old tax havens have adopted the more benign designation of *offshore financial centre* (OFC) and tend to describe themselves as financial centres specializing in non-residential financial transactions. However, with their array of secrecy provisions that lack regulation, zero or near zero taxation imposed by them, and lack of adequate capital controls, they are logical extensions of the traditional tax havens. The International Monetary Fund (IMF) has defined OFCs as centres where the bulk of financial sector transactions on both sides of the balance sheet are with individuals or companies that are not residents, where the transactions are initiated elsewhere, and where the majority of the institutions involved are controlled by non-residents. Thus, many OFCs have the following characteristics:

1. Jurisdictions that have financial institutions engaged primarily in business with non-residents.
2. Financial systems with external assets and liabilities out of proportion to domestic financial intermediation.
3. Centres which provide some or all of the following opportunities: (a) low or zero taxation, (b) moderate or light financial regulation, and (c) banking secrecy and anonymity.

Various studies on tax havens have shown that tax havens are typically small countries/jurisdictions, with low or nil taxation for foreigners who decide to come and settle there. They usually also offer strong confidentiality or secrecy regarding wealth and accounts, making them very attractive locations for safe keeping of unaccounted wealth. They also offer a very liberal regulatory environment and allow opaque existence, where an entity can easily be set up without indulging in any meaningful commercial activity and yet claim to be a genuine business unit, merely by getting itself incorporated or registered in that jurisdiction. This makes them highly desirable locations for multinational entities wishing to reduce their global tax liabilities.

These multinational entities—consisting of a network of several corporate and non-corporate bodies—may set up conduit companies in tax havens and artificially transfer their income to such conduit companies in view of the low tax regime there. There is increasing global awareness and concern about the role of tax havens and their facilitation of certain abusive and undesirable arrangements that result in significant fiscal challenges to other countries and also pose a threat in terms of potential financing of terrorism and other activities that threaten peace and security.

The role of tax havens has gradually come under scrutiny globally. With near-zero tax regimes, banking secrecy, and weak financial regulations, these tax havens facilitate hiding of money accumulated through tax evasion and other illegal means in addition to creating risks of terrorist financing and money laundering. At the G-7 summit in Lyons in 1996, a call was given to the OECD to prepare a report to address these issues with a view to establishing a multilateral approach under which countries could operate individually and collectively to limit the extent of these practices. The OECD came up with a report in 1998 and called for action against tax havens. The report envisaged blacklisting of and internationally coordinated sanctions against havens that persisted in luring other states' tax bases.

3.6 Participatory Notes (PNs)

A participatory note (PN) is a derivative instrument issued in foreign jurisdictions, by a foreign institutional investor (FII)/or one of its associates, against underlying Indian securities.

PNs are popular among foreign investors since they allow these investors to earn returns on investment in the Indian market without undergoing the significant cost and time implications of directly investing in India. These instruments are traded overseas outside the direct purview of Securities and Exchange Board of India (SEBI) surveillance thereby raising many apprehensions about the beneficial ownership and the nature of funds invested in these instruments. Concerns have been raised that some of the money coming into the market via PNs could be the unaccounted wealth camouflaged under the guise of FII investment. SEBI has been taking measures to ensure that PNs are not used as conduits for black money or terrorist funding.

3.7 Investment through Complex Derivative Instruments

With increasing sophistication of derivative instruments [2], new opportunities for investing and making profits without being subjected to taxes and regulations are also opening up. Such innovative means can also be misused by unscrupulous parties to generate unaccounted income. Some such instruments like participatory notes may not be adequately covered by regulatory mechanisms and their oversight and hence have potential for misuse.

End Notes

1. Agricultural income is exempt from tax under Section 10 (1) of the Income Tax Act, 1961.
2. Derivative in mathematics means a variable derived from another variable. The term *derivative* indicates that it has no independent value, i.e. its value is entirely *derived* from the value of the underlying asset. The underlying asset can be security, commodity, bullion, currency, live stock or anything else. In other words, derivative means a forward, future, option or any other hybrid contract of pre-determined fixed duration, linked for the purpose of contract fulfilment to the value of a specified real or financial asset of an index of securities. Similarly, in the financial sense, a derivative is a financial product, which has been derived from a market for another product. Without the underlying product, derivatives do not have any independent existence in the market.
   Derivative instruments are defined by the Indian Securities Contracts (Regulation) Act, 1956 to include: (a) a security derived from a debt instrument, share, secured/unsecured loan, risk instrument or contract for differences, or any other form of security, and (b) a contract that derives its value from the

prices/index of prices of underlying securities.

In other words, derivatives are financial instruments/contracts whose value depends upon the value of an underlying. Since their value is essentially derived out of an underlying, they are financial abstractions whose value is derived mathematically from the changes in the value of the underlying.

The International Monetary Fund (IMF) defines derivatives as "financial instruments that are linked to a specific financial instrument or indicator or commodity and through which specific financial risks can be traded in financial markets in their own right. The value of a financial derivative derives from the price of an underlying item, such as an asset or index. Unlike debt securities, no principal is advanced to be repaid and no investment income accrues".

4

Estimates of Black Money/Tax Evasion

Since black money is unaccounted for, there are no reliable estimates of it. Similarly, there is no well-defined and universally acceptable methodology for estimation of black money. Hence, all attempts at its estimation have produced results with wide variations. Several estimates have been floated—often without adequate factual basis—on the magnitude of black money generated in the country and the unaccounted wealth stashed aboard.

4.1 Black Money: Estimation Techniques

4.1.1 Input-output Method [1]: It consists of using the input/output ratio along with the input to calculate the true output. It estimates black money as the difference between the declared output and the output expected on the basis of the input/output ratio. This method is deceptively simple and, though it may have some utility if applied to a uniform industry or a specific sector of the economy, it is unlikely to be of much help if applied to economy as a whole. It also ignores structural changes in the economy including those related to technology.

4.1.2 Money Circulation Approach: Another approach, adopted by the monetarists, is based on the fact that money is needed to circulate incomes in both the *black* and accounted for economies. As the official economy is known, the difference between that amount and the money in circulation could be assumed to be the circulating *black* component. An estimate of the velocity of money [2] enables an estimation of income circulated annually. A comparison of that with the income captured in the National Accounting System (NAS) gives the income which could be estimated as the black money in the economy. However, the assumption that the NAS represents accounted incomes accurately is not always true. Large proportions of income, such as those falling in the unorganized sector, are not accurately captured in NAS.

4.1.3 Survey Method: Under it, sample surveys are carried out for estimation of black money. These may be on the consumption pattern of a representative population sample, which is then compared to the total consumption of the country. In this method, the problems consist in getting a truly representative sample, and the willingness of persons in the sample size to reveal true facts. As is well-known, people are often unwilling to reveal their *true state of affairs* and admit any illegality before surveyors.

4.2 Various Estimates of Black Money/Tax Evasion

Widespread tax evasion is a perennial problem of the Indian tax system. The history of taxation law amendments in India is essentially a history of plugging loopholes, as and when discovered, to prevent leakages of revenue.

4.2.1 Early Attempts: The problem of tax evasion and generation of black money is not new. As far back as 1936, the Ayers Committee, while reviewing the income tax administration in India suggested large-scale amendments to secure the interests of the honest taxpayer and effectively deal with fraudulent evasion.

The Income Tax Investigation Commission was appointed in 1947 to investigate tax evasion and suggest measures for preventing it in future.

Soon after Independence in 1947, the Indian Income Tax Investigation Commission, 1948, investigated all matters relating to taxation of income, with particular reference to preventing evasion and avoidance. The Commission recommended several changes in the law to plug loopholes in the income tax system. It recommended, *inter alia*, that the law should be amended so as to allow speculative losses to be set off only against speculative gains.

Since early 1950s, various commissions, committees and individual scholars have made estimates of tax evasion in India, particularly evasion of income tax. The findings of these studies are summarised below chronologically.

4.2.2 Taxation Enquiry Commission (TEC) [Chairman: John Matthai], 1953-54: TEC which dealt at length with the administration of income tax, found staggering levels of tax evasion. To quote, "It is observed from statistics in connection with the Disclosure Drive that income as originally included in the returns sent to the income tax department by assessees who made disclosures was grossly understated, the difference between the income as originally returned and that disclosed later to the department being, on the average, as much as 600 percent. Such other statistics as have been made available to us by the Central Board of Revenue also give evidence of the fact that evasion is prevalent on a considerable scale". [3] The Commission maintained that improvement and strengthening of the enforcement machinery was the only way to tackle evasion effectively.

4.2.3 Estimates of Nicholas Kaldor: Nicholas Kaldor, a British economist, made the first systematic estimates of income tax evasion in India in the mid-1950s. He estimated income tax loss through tax evasion at ₹ 200 to ₹ 300 crore for the year 1953-54. [4] The estimates of Kaldor were based on certain tentative figures relating to national income provided to him by the Central Statistical Organisation (CSO). Kaldor made it clear in his report that his estimates were tentative and should be interpreted with caution. His recommendations resulted in several amendments to the Income Tax Act and new legislations like the Wealth Tax Act.

4.2.4 Central Board of Revenue: Another study by the Central Board of Revenue for the same year (1953-54) recorded a much lower estimate of tax evasion at ₹ 20 to ₹ 30 crore, almost one-tenth of Kaldor's estimate. [5] One main reason for the wide divergence between the two estimates was the inclusion in Kaldor's estimate of what the Central Board of

Revenue counted as avoidance rather than evasion. Kaldor himself had admitted while tendering oral evidence before Direct Taxes Administration Enquiry Committee, 1958-59, that his estimate represented the loss of tax not only through evasion but also through avoidance. [6] Therefore, it is generally agreed that the estimates of income tax evasion by Kaldor were on the high side.

4.2.5 Direct Taxes Enquiry Committee (DTEC) [Chairman: Justice K.N. Wanchoo], 1971: DTEC [7] was appointed in 1971 to examine and suggest legal and administrative measures for unearthing black money and countering evasion and checking avoidance. It comprehensively dealt with the causes of and methods of tackling tax evasion and made a number of recommendations for strengthening tax administration.

It estimated assessable non-salary income for the year 1961-62 at ₹ 2,686 crore and non-salary income actually assessed to tax to be of the order of ₹ 1,875 crore. Accordingly the income which escaped income tax was of the order of ₹ 811 crore. After making rough adjustments for exemptions and deductions, the Wanchoo Committee found that 'the estimated income on which tax has been evaded (black income) would probably be ₹ 700 crore and ₹ 1,000 crore for the years 1961-62 and 1965-66 respectively'. 'Projecting this estimate further to 1968-69 on the basis of percentage increase in national income from 1961-62 to 1968-69, the income on which tax was evaded for 1968-69 was estimated as ₹ 1,800 crore'.

4.2.6 National Institute of Public Finance and Policy (NIPFP): In its study conducted in 1985, NIPFP defined *black money* as the aggregate of incomes which were taxable but which were not reported to tax authorities. The study made use of a range rather than a single figure of underestimation. While preparing the estimate of *black* income, the study excluded incomes generated through illegal activities like smuggling, black market transactions, and acceptance of bribes and kickbacks.

NIPFP study estimated the ratio of tax-evaded income to GDP in the range of 3.7 percent to 5.7 percent in 1975-76, and 4.2 percent to 8.6 percent in 1980-81. [8]

4.2.7 Tax Reforms Committee (TRC) [Chairman: Raja Chelliah], 1991: According to TRC, "not more than 30-35 percent of legally taxable income is being disclosed, on the average". [9] In this context it observed, "it would be fair to say that the income tax department which is in-charge of all the Central Government direct taxes is in shambles. It cannot complain of lack of manpower, but the majority of personnel is constituted by inspectors and clerks who are not adequately trained and are paid fairly low salaries". [10]

Apart from the foregoing estimates, some evidence of general nature also suggests widespread non-reporting and under-reporting of taxable income in India. In this connection, the Finance Minister in his 1997-98 budget speech observed, "It is inexplicable that in a country of over 900 million people, only 12 million people are assessed to income tax and what is worse, only about 12,000 assessees are in the tax bracket of income above ₹ 10 lakh". [11]

It is noteworthy that tax evasion is not confined to income tax only, rather it is widely practised for other direct taxes also like wealth tax. The ridiculously low yield from these taxes is partly due to plethora of exemptions/concessions and also due to widespread evasion. In India, economic inequalities have been caused mainly by the inequitable ownership of wealth and the failure of the wealth tax to make a headway in lessening inequalities is indeed regrettable.

It may be recalled that in 1957 and 1958, three new taxes were introduced, viz. wealth tax, expenditure tax, and gift tax. Estate duty was already in operation since 1953. The basic philosophy underlying the introduction of the system of integrated direct taxes was to prevent evasion and avoidance of direct taxes and thereby to reduce inequalities of income and wealth. However, the yield from wealth tax, expenditure tax, gift tax, and estate duty has never been of much significance in the Central tax structure. The meagre revenue collection ultimately led to the abolition of expenditure tax, estate duty and gift tax in 1966, 1985 and 1998 respectively. Wealth tax continues to be in operation.

Wealth tax liability is computed by applying the rate schedule to net wealth (i.e. taxable wealth). Presently (financial year 2013-14), wealth tax is charged at the flat rate of 1 percent in the case of all assessees having taxable wealth exceeding ₹ 30 lakh. In view of the meagre revenue and problems of administration and compliance, the Task Force on Direct Taxes (Chairman: Vijay Kelkar), 2002 recommended the abolition of wealth tax.

Estimation of evasion of indirect taxes in India has always remained a hard task even for the officially appointed committees. For example, the Central Excise (Self-Removal Procedure) Review Committee, 1973, made extensive studies of excise evasion, both sector-wise and commodity-wise. However, it could not quantify the total magnitude of evasion. It observed, "we have reached the conclusion that evasion is considerable and, in certain sectors, pervasive. This is an inference we have drawn from the totality of what we have seen, heard and investigated." [12]

As regards black money stashed abroad, the White Paper on Black Money observed, "It is however useful to mention here one estimate of the amount of Indian deposits in Swiss banks (located in Switzerland) which has been made by the Swiss National Bank. Its spokesperson stated that at the end of 2010, the total liabilities of Swiss Banks towards Indians were 1.945 billion Swiss Francs (about ₹ 9,295 crore). The Swiss Ministry of External Affairs confirmed these figures when a reference was made by the Indian Ministry of External Affairs to them". [13] The White Paper further noted, "The illicit money transferred outside India may come back to India through various methods such as hawala, mis-pricing, foreign direct investment (FDI) through beneficial tax jurisdictions, raising of capital by Indian companies through global depository receipts (GDRs), and investment in Indian stock markets through participatory notes. It is possible that a large amount of money transferred outside India might actually have returned through these means". [14]

End Notes

1. Input-output analysis, attributed to American economist Wassily Loentief, examines the interdependence of the production plans and activities of the various industries which constitute an economy. This interdependence arises because each industry employs the outputs of other industries, and its own output in turn is used by other industries. For example, steel is used to make railway wagons and railway wagons are in turn used to transport steel.
   An input-output transaction matrix is a framework of data which provides a detailed information on how the final demand for output is related to the requirements placed on individual industries. It thus, highlights the interdependence of various economic sectors (industries) in the production of final output for the economy as a whole.
2. Money in an economy consists partly of currency and partly of bank deposits. The currency and bank deposits that actually circulate are used over and over again in the course of a specified period (say one year). Every time they are used they enter into a price. Therefore, the total amount of purchasing power which enters into the price level depends on the flow (rather than the stock) of money. The flow can be considered in terms of the stock if the latter is multiplied by its velocity of circulation which is defined as the average number of times a unit of money changes hands during the course of one year. If M is the stock of money and V its velocity of circulation, then the flow of money will be MV.
3. Government of India, Ministry of Finance, *Report of the Taxation Enquiry Commission* (Chairman, John Matthai), 1953-54, Volume II, p. 189.
4. Nicholas Kaldor, *Indian Tax Reform: Report of a Survey* (Government of India, Ministry of Finance, 1956), p. 105.
5. Quoted by Government of India, Ministry of Finance, *Report of the Direct Taxes Administration Enquiry Committee* (Chairman: Mahavir Tyagi), 1958-59, p. 148.

6. *Ibid.*, p. 148.
7. Government of India, Ministry of Finance, *Final Report of Direct Taxes Enquiry Committee* (Chairman, Justice K.N. Wanchoo), December 1971.
8. Government of India, Ministry of Finance, *Aspects of the Black Economy in India*, March 1985, p. 161.
9. Government of India, Ministry of Finance, *Interim Report of the Tax Reforms Committee* (Chairman, Raja Chelliah), December 1991, p. 47.
10. *Ibid.*, p. 37.
11. Government of India, Ministry of Finance, *Budget 1997-98, Speech of the Finance Minister*, Part B, p. 25.
12. Government of India, Ministry of Finance, *Report of the Central Excise (Self-Removal Procedure) Review Committee* (Chairman, B. Venkatappiah), 1973, p. 65.
13. Government of India, Ministry of Finance, *White Paper on Black Money,* May 2012, para 2.6.4.
14. *Ibid.*, para 2.4.9.

5

Institutional Structure to Deal with Black Money/Tax Evasion

The responsibility of dealing with the challenge of unaccounted wealth and its consequences is jointly and collectively shared by a number of institutions belonging to the Central and State Governments. These various organisations closely monitor violation of laws regulating economic activities and their links with other criminal activities and in doing so provide a comprehensive network of checks and balances against generation of black money too. However, the federal structure of governance and their vertical reporting systems within their respective ministries and departments may have resulted in less than optimum coordination of data, information, and actions and a strengthening of this aspect may be an important way forward in the fight against generation and accumulation of black money.

5.1 Agencies for Enforcement of Tax Laws

5.1.1 Central Board of Direct Taxes (CBDT): The CBDT, New Delhi, is part of the Department of Revenue in the Ministry of Finance. While the CBDT provides essential inputs for policy and planning of direct taxes in India, it is also responsible for administration of direct tax laws through its Income Tax Department. The CBDT is a statutory authority functioning under the Central Board of Revenue Act, 1963. The officials of the Board in their ex-officio capacity also function as a Division of the Ministry dealing with matters relating to the levy and collection of direct taxes.

The Income Tax Department is primarily responsible for combating the menace of black money. For this purpose, it uses the tools of scrutiny assessment as well as information-based investigations for detecting tax evasion and penalising the same as per provisions of the Income Tax Act, 1961 with the objective of creating deterrence against tax evasion. In doing so, it plays one of the most important roles in preventing generation, accumulation, and consumption of unaccounted black money.

The Investigation Wing of the Income Tax Department deals with investigations to detect tax evasion and carries out operations like surveys and searches to collect evidence of such evasion. Such operations are usually carried out after detailed preliminary investigations and in cases involving substantial evasion of taxes.

A. Directorate of Criminal Investigation (DCI): Till recently, the tax administration in India did not have a separate set-up for targeted investigation into criminal cases. On May 30, 2011, a notification was issued by the Government of India for creation of a Directorate of Income Tax (Criminal Investigation) or DCI in the Central Board of Direct Taxes, Department of Revenue, Ministry of Finance. The DCI is mandated to perform functions in respect of criminal matters having any financial implication punishable as an offence under any direct taxes law.

The DCI, in discharge of its responsibilities under the direct tax laws, is required to perform the following functions:

1. Seek and collect information about persons and transactions suspected to be involved in criminal activities having cross-border, inter-state, or international ramifications that pose a threat to national security and are punishable under the direct tax laws.
2. Investigate the sources and uses of funds involved in such criminal activities.
3. Cause issuance of show cause notices for offences committed under any direct tax law.
4. File prosecution complaints in the competent court under any direct tax law relating to a criminal activity.
5. Hire the services of special prosecutors and other experts

for pursuing a prosecution complaint filed in any court of competent jurisdiction.

6. Execute appropriate witness protection programmes for effective prosecution of criminal offences under the direct tax laws, i.e. to protect and rehabilitate witnesses who support the state in prosecution of such offences so as to insulate them from any harm to their person.
7. Coordinate with and extend necessary expert, technical, and logistical support to any other intelligence or law enforcement agency in India investigating crimes having cross-border, inter-state or international ramifications that pose a threat to national security.
8. Enter into agreements for sharing of information and other cooperation with any central or state agency in India.
9. Enter into agreements for sharing of information and other cooperation with such agencies of foreign states as may be permissible under any international agreement or treaty.
10. Any other matter relating to the above.

The DCI is headed by a Director General of Income Tax (Criminal Investigation) and functions under administrative control of the CBDT. The head office of the DCI is located at New Delhi and it has eight regional offices all over India.

B. Exchange of Information (EoI) Cell: The Government of India has set up an EoI Cell in CBDT. The EoI works on the basis of mutual cooperation. The competent authorities of different countries provide different forms of administrative assistance to each other based on the provisions of Double Tax Avoidance Agreements (DTAAs) or the Multilateral Convention for Mutual Administrative Assistance. Administrative assistance under these instruments of EOI, depending on the terms of the agreement, may take the form of: (a) specific exchange of information, (b) spontaneous exchange of information, (c) automatic exchange of information, (d) tax examination abroad, (e) simultaneous exchange of information, (f) service of documents, and (g) assistance in collection of tax.

C. Income Tax Overseas Units (ITOUs): With increased

scope for international cooperation in areas of exchange of information, transfer pricing, and taxation of cross-border transactions, Government of India decided to create a network of ITOUs. In addition to the existing two ITOUs at Singapore and Mauritius, eight more have been opened. The objectives of these ITOUs are as under:

1. Monitor DTAA-related issues.
2. Assist the authorities in handling issues arising out of international taxation and transfer pricing.
3. Assist the authorities in frequent revision of existing DTAAs.
4. Assist the authorities in negotiation of TIEAs.
5. Expedite the exchange of information by the competent authorities (as per DTAAs and TIEAs) of these countries as required by the competent authority in India.
6. Assist the authorities in collection of taxes.
7. Assist the authorities in work relating to Mutual Agreement Procedure under DTAAs.
8. Maintain liaison with various departments of the respective countries especially income tax department, registrar of companies, department of banking services, and administrators of financial services.
9. Maintain liaison with investors investing in India from these countries.
10. Impart information about domestic laws of India to foreign investors.
11. Maintain liaison with Indian investors in these countries to assess any tax-related problems arising for these investors.
12. Assist the Mission in any other commercial/economic work assigned to the officer by the Head of the Mission.
13. Any other work assigned to the officer by the CBDT, Department of Revenue.

Opening of the new ITOUs and presence of tax officers in the ITOUs also acts as effective deterrence against tax evasion.

5.1.2 Central Board of Excise and Customs (CBEC): The CBEC is a part of the Department of Revenue under the

Ministry of Finance, Government of India. It deals with the tasks of formulation of policy concerning levy and collection of customs and central excise duties, prevention of smuggling, and administration of matters relating to customs, central excise and narcotics to the extent under the CBEC's purview. The Board is the administrative authority for its subordinate organizations, including Custom Houses, Central Excise Commissionerates, and the Central Revenues Control Laboratory.

The Directorate General of Central Excise Intelligence (DGCEI) is the apex intelligence organization functioning under the CBEC. It is entrusted with the responsibility of detecting cases of evasion of central excise and service tax. The Directorate develops intelligence, especially in new areas of tax evasion through its intelligence network across the country and disseminates information in this respect by issuing modus operandi circulars and alert circulars to apprise field formations of the latest trends in duty evasion. Wherever found necessary, DGCEI on its own, or in coordination with field formations, organises operations to unearth evasion of central excise duty and service tax.

5.2 Regulatory Authorities for Supervision and Policing

5.2.1 Central Bureau of Investigation (CBI): CBI, functioning under the Department of Personnel, Ministry of Personnel, Pension and Public Grievances, Government of India, is the premier investigating police agency in India. It handles a broad category of criminal cases including cases of corruption and fraud committed by public servants, economic crimes, and other specific crimes involving terrorism, bomb blasts, sensational homicides, kidnappings and the underworld. The CBI plays an important role in international cooperation relating to mutual legal assistance and extradition matters. The Ministry of Home Affairs is the central authority for mutual legal assistance in criminal matters and the Ministry of External Affairs, the nodal agency for extradition matters.

5.2.2 Financial Intelligence Unit (FIU): The FIU-IND was established by the Government of India on November 18, 2004 for coordinating and strengthening efforts for national and international intelligence by investigation and enforcement agencies in combating money laundering and terrorist financing. FIU-IND is the national agency responsible for receiving, processing, analysing, and disseminating information relating to suspect financial transactions. It is an independent body reporting to the Economic Intelligence Council headed by the Finance Minister. For administrative purposes, the FIU-IND is under the control of the Department of Revenue, Ministry of Finance.

5.2.3 Narcotics Control Bureau (NCB): It functions under the Ministry of Home Affairs, Government of India. It was established on March 17, 1986 and its functions include co-ordination of actions by various offices, state governments, and other authorities under the Narcotics Drugs and Psychotropic Substances (NDPS) Act, 1985, Customs Act, Drugs and Cosmetics Act, and any other law for the time being in force in connection with the enforcement provisions of the NDPS Act. It is assigned the task of counter measures against illicit drugs traffic under the various international conventions and protocols, and also assists concerned authorities in foreign countries and concerned international organisations dealing with prevention and suppression of this traffic.

5.3 Co-ordinating Agencies

5.3.1 Central Economic Intelligence Bureau (CEIB): The CEIB functioning under the Ministry of Finance is responsible for coordination, intelligence sharing, and investigations at national as well as regional levels amongst various law enforcement agencies. The existing coordination mechanism in the CEIB consists of Regional Economic Intelligence Councils (REICs) at regional level and the Group on Economic Intelligence and meetings of the heads of investigating agencies under the Department of Revenue at the centre. While the Group on Economic Intelligence is focused on matters relating to intelligence sharing, the REICs and heads of agencies meetings cover both intelligence and investigations.

5.3.2 National Investigation Agency (NIA): It is a specialised and dedicated investigating agency set up under the National Investigation Agency Act to investigate and prosecute scheduled offences, in particular offences under the Unlawful Activities (Prevention) Act, including financing of terrorism. The NIA has concurrent jurisdiction with the individual states, thereby empowering the Central Government to probe terror attacks in any part of the country. Officers of the NIA have all powers, privileges, and liabilities which police officers have in connection with investigation of an offence.

The Central Government has the power to suo moto assign a case to the NIA for investigation. The NIA Act also provides for setting up of special courts and trials to be held on a day-to-day basis. The NIA Act can investigate offences under the specific Acts mentioned in the Schedule to NIA Act, including the Atomic Energy Act, 1962; Unlawful Activities (Prevention) Act, 1967; Anti-Hijacking Act, 1982; Suppression of Unlawful Acts against Safety of Civil Aviation Act, 1982; SAARC Convention (Suppression of Terrorism) Act, 1993; Suppression of Unlawful Acts against Safety of Maritime Navigation and Fixed Platforms on Continental Shelf Act, 2002; Weapons of Mass Destruction and Their Delivery Systems (Prohibition of Unlawful Activities) Act, 2005; and offences under Chapter VI and Sections 489-A to 489-E of the Indian Penal Code.

5.4 Other Agencies

5.4.1 Central Bureau of Narcotics (CBN): It supervises the cultivation of opium poppy in India and issues necessary licences for manufacture, export and import of narcotics drugs and psychotropic substances. It monitors India's implementation of the United Nations Drug Control Conventions and also interacts with the International Narcotics Control Board (INCB) in Vienna and the competent authorities of other countries to verify the genuineness of a transaction prior to authorising shipments.

5.4.2 Serious Frauds Investigation Office (SFIO): It functions under the Ministry of Corporate Affairs and takes up for investigation complex cases having inter-departmental and multidisciplinary ramifications and substantial involvement of public interest, either in terms of monetary misappropriation or in terms of persons affected. It also takes up cases where investigation has the potential of contributing towards a clear improvement in systems, laws, or procedures.

5.4.3 Registrar of Companies (RoCs): It is the Registry for companies and limited liability firms and is established under the Ministry of Corporate Affairs. The Ministry of Corporate Affairs has a three-tier organisational set-up consisting of a Secretariat in New Delhi, Regional Directorates in Mumbai, Kolkata, Chennai and Noida, and field offices in all states and union territories.

5.4.4 Registrar of Societies (RoSs): The Registrars of non-profit societies are within State Government's purview and most of the states have a RoS office. The Society Registration Act is a Central Act but many states have adopted it with some state amendments and are registering non-profit societies under their respective Acts. Some state assemblies have enacted completely separate legislation on the subject. The RoS offices are reservoirs of data on societies and also function as their regulator.

5.4.5 Economic Intelligence Council (EIC): It came into existence in 2003 and is chaired by the Finance Minister and comprises senior functionaries of various ministries and intelligence agencies, including the Governor of the Reserve Bank of India (RBI) and the Chairman of Securities and Exchange Board of India (SEBI). The EIC meets at least once a year to discuss and take decisions regarding trends in economic offences and strategies on intelligence sharing, coordination etc. The implementation of decisions taken by the EIC is monitored by the Working Group on Intelligence Apparatus, set up for this purpose within the EIC.

5.4.6 National Crime Records Bureau (NCRB): It was set up with the objective of empowering the Indian police services with information technology and criminal intelligence with a view to enabling them to effectively and efficiently enforce the law. It therefore, creates and maintains a secured national database on crimes, criminals, property, and organised criminal gangs for use by law enforcement agencies.

The NCRB also processes and disseminates fingerprint records of criminals, including foreign criminals, to establish their identity.

5.4.7 State Police Agencies: Under the Constitution of India, police and public order are state (provincial) subjects. Every State/Union Territory has its own police force, which performs not only normal policing duties but also has specialised units to combat economic offences. The Economic Offences Wing (EOW) of the police functioning under the administrative control of states (provinces) is entrusted with the responsibility of investigation of serious economic offences and offences having inter-state ramifications.

6

Measures Adopted to Curb Black Money/Tax Evasion

Direct Taxes Enquiry Committee (Chairman: Justice K.N. Wanchoo), 1971, had suggested various measures to fight the evil of black money and tax evasion. Some of the measures suggested were as follows.

1. Reduction in tax rates.
2. Minimisation of controls and licences.
3. Regulation of donations to political parties.
4. Creating confidence among small taxpayers.
5. Substitution of sales tax by excise duty.
6. Vigorous prosecution policy.
7. Compulsory maintenance of accounts.

To give effect to the recommendations made by the Committee, the Government enacted the Taxation Laws (Amendment) Act, 1975. This Act, *inter alia,* provided stringent punishment for tax evaders. In cases where tax evasion exceeded ₹ 1 lakh or prosecution was for the second or subsequent offence, the maximum punishment prescribed was 7 years rigorous imprisonment. Also, the discretionary powers to courts to award monetary punishment as an alternative to imprisonment or to reduce the term of imprisonment less than the minimum period, was withdrawn.

Efforts have been made to curb tax evasion and control black money through various measures: Some of these are described below.

1. Lowering of tax rates.
2. Tax amnesties.
3. Advance tax payment.
4. Withholding tax [or tax deduction at source (TDS)].
5. Presumptive tax for small traders.

6. Permanent account number (PAN) or general index register number (GIR).
7. Survey of income tax.
8. Summons, and search and seizure.
9. Penalties and prosecutions.
10. Use of information technology (IT) in tax administration.

6.1 Lowering of Tax Rates

The Report of the Direct Taxes Enquiry Committee (DTEC), 1971, was a milestone in the area of income tax rates. The Committee made a number of far-reaching suggestions for unearthing black money, preventing evasion and avoidance of taxes, and reducing arrears. One important recommendation of the Committee related to reduction in the rates of direct taxes which in its view were mainly responsible for tax evasion because they made tax evasion profitable and attractive. The rates of individual income tax were quite high till the year 1973-74. These high rates, necessitated by contingencies like drought and war, when combined with the prevailing shortages, resulted in controls and licences, and thereby provided further incentives for evasion of taxes. It was largely in this economic environment that generation of black money became highly prevalent and acquired serious proportions.

However, pursuant to the recommendations of the DTEC, the Government initiated a series of rate reductions in individual income tax. The top marginal rate of tax was reduced from 97.7 percent in 1973-74 to 77 percent in 1974-75, and further down to 66 percent in 1976-77. It is noteworthy that DTEC had recommended a maximum marginal rate of 75 percent. [1]

The downward trend in the rate of income tax was temporarily reversed during the brief Janata Government rule at the Centre. The top marginal rate of income tax was increased from 66 percent in 1976-77 to 69 percent in 1977-78, and further up to 72 percent in 1979-80. However, the policy of low direct tax rates started by the Congress

Government in 1974 and carried forward in 1976 was further reinforced after it came back to power at the Centre in 1980. After a series of revisions, the maximum marginal rate of individual income tax was 54 percent (including employment surcharge of 8 percent), applicable from the financial year 1990-91.

Consequent upon the recommendations contained in the Interim Report of the Tax Reforms Committee (Chairman: Raja Chelliah), 1991, the top marginal rate was fixed at 44.8 percent (including surcharge) from the financial year 1992-93. The Finance Act, 1994 abolished the surcharge of 12 percent and hence the maximum marginal rate of tax was 40 percent from the financial year 1994-95. From the same year it was made applicable on incomes over ₹ 1,20,000. It may be recalled that the top marginal rate of income tax applied to incomes above ₹ 1 lakh from 1967-68 to 1993-94. The ₹ 1 lakh of 1967-68 was approximately equivalent to ₹ 5.5 lakh of 1993-94. This showed the laxity of the administration in adjusting tax brackets for inflation. It is noteworthy that Tax Reforms Committee had recommended 40 percent maximum rate inclusive of surcharge for income exceeding ₹ 2 lakh.

The maximum marginal rate of personal income tax was further reduced from 40 percent to 30 percent in the 1997-98 budget. In another significant move, it was made applicable to incomes above ₹ 1,50,000. Presently (financial year 2013-14), the top marginal rate of 30 percent is applicable on income above ₹ 10 lakh in the case of individuals.

Low tax rates are welcome provided they improve compliance and revenue yield. However, to expect that lowering of rates would improve compliance automatically is unrealistic because tax evasion occurs at all levels of income. As the Indian Direct Taxation Administration Enquiry Committee, 1958-59, observed, "While we cannot deny that the higher the rate of tax, the greater will be the temptation for evasion and avoidance, we feel that the tax rates by themselves are not to blame for the large extent of evasion in the country.

Even if the rates of tax are reduced, evasion will still continue, because it exists at all levels of income". [2]

6.2 Tax Amnesties

Government may provide opportunity, from time to time, to tax evaders to declare their past concealments of income and wealth without fear of being prosecuted. Tax amnesty (or impunity) is granted only for the past in order to secure better compliance and thus higher tax yield in the present and future. Tax amnesties (or voluntary disclosure schemes) bring concealed money in the open, broaden the base of investment and hence accelerate economic development.

However, tax amnesties are criticized on the grounds that they provide a premium on dishonesty and are unfair to honest taxpayers. Tax amnesties set bad precedents and encourage tax evaders in the hope that they will be let off leniently for their past sins any time in the future. Practically, the same group of tax evaders takes advantage of tax amnesties announced by the government. The honest taxpayers are demoralised and the tax enforcement machinery also loses respect in the eyes of the common man.

In India, tax amnesties with varied characteristics have been offered from time to time to unearth black money. These amnesties provided taxpayers immunity from interest, penalty, investigation or prosecution in exchange for disclosures of incomes which did not pay tax.

In 1951, a voluntary disclosure scheme was announced under which penal provisions of tax laws were relaxed to persuade tax evaders to disclose their unaccounted incomes.

Under another scheme, announced in 1965, tax evaders were required to pay 60 percent of the disclosed income by way of tax and allowed to bring into books of account the remaining 40 percent.

Another scheme announced in 1975 provided for clubbing together of all black income irrespective of the years over which it was earned and treated as a block separately from other taxable income for the purpose of income tax liability. It provided for a concessional rate of tax ranging from 25 percent to 60 percent on income disclosed under the scheme.

6.2.1 Special Bearer Bonds: In 1981, Government offered Special Bearer Bonds to the public. The Bonds were redeemable after 10 years (i.e. in 1991) and carried 2 percent per annum simple rate of interest. The Bonds were marketable and the holders were not required to explain their origin. On their redemption, the holders were allowed to bring them into their books. The value of the Bonds and interest thereon were exempt from income tax and wealth tax till their redemption.

6.2.2 Voluntary Deposit Scheme, 1991: This scheme to mobilise unaccounted money was announced through the Voluntary Deposits (Immunities and Exemptions) Act, 1991. Under this scheme, any person could make a deposit with the National Housing Bank on or before January 31, 1992. Thereupon, 40 percent of such deposit was deducted and set apart as a special levy for financing slum clearance and low cost housing for the poor. The balance of 60 percent was credited to the depositor's account which he was allowed to withdraw in one or more instalments for any purpose specified by him. Persons who made deposits under this scheme were not required to disclose the sources of funds from which the deposits were made. Hence, the money deposited was completely immune from all sorts of inquiry and investigation.

6.2.3 Gold Bond Scheme, 1993: This scheme was introduced through the Gold Bonds (Immunities and Exemptions) Ordinance, 1993, promulgated by the President on January 31, 1993. The objective of the scheme was to mobilise idle gold reserves of the country to supplement official reserves and thereby strengthen the credit position of the country in the international market. The scheme allowed amnesty from the provisions of direct tax laws to induce persons to legitimise their unaccounted holding of gold.

The scheme remained open for subscription from March 15, 1993 to June 14, 1993. Subscription to the Gold Bonds was made in the form of gold only. The minimum limit for subscription was 500 grams of gold. There was no maximum limit. A subscriber was not required to disclose, for any purpose whatsoever, the nature and source of acquisition of the gold subscribed for the Gold Bonds, including the money with which the gold was acquired.

The Bonds matured after 5 years from the date of issue and were repaid in the form of gold. Besides, a lump sum interest of ₹ 40 per gram of gold for the period of 5 years was paid on maturity.

6.2.4 Voluntary Disclosure of Income Scheme (VDIS), 1997: In his 1997-98 budget speech, the Finance Minister announced the introduction of a Voluntary Disclosure Scheme to harness black money for productive purposes. The scheme was rechristened as Voluntary Disclosure of Income Scheme, 1997 by the Finance Minister while moving amendments to the Finance Bill in the Lok Sabha on May 7, 1997.

VDIS, 1997 announced by the Central Board of Direct Taxes on June 18, 1997 had the following provisions.

1. The scheme came into force from July 1, 1997. Any eligible person could make a disclosure of income on or after this date. The last date for making the disclosure was December 31, 1997. Thus, the scheme lasted for six months.
2. A person could make a disclosure in respect of income chargeable to tax under the Indian Income Tax Act, 1961 for any assessment year.
3. The particulars furnished by a declarant were kept a secret. Nothing contained in any declaration was used against the declarant for the purpose of any proceedings relating to imposition of penalties or launching of prosecution under the Income Tax Act, 1961, Wealth Tax Act, 1957, Foreign Exchange Regulation Act, 1973 or the Companies Act, 1956.
4. The tax payable on the disclosed income in respect of any assessment year was at the rate of 35 percent in the case of

companies and 30 percent in the case of other assessees including individuals.

5. The tax payable under the scheme was to be paid before the filing of the declaration. In other words, the declaration was accompanied by the proof of payment of tax. In case a person was not in a position to pay the tax before the filing of the declaration, he was allowed to do so within three months of the date of filing of the declaration. In such a case, a simple interest at the rate of 2 percent was charged for every month or part of a month beginning from the date of filing of the declaration to the date of payment of the tax.
6. The declaration was made to the Commissioner of Income Tax in his area and was in a prescribed format. The declaration was signed in the case of an individual by the individual himself. In the case of a hindu undivided family, company, firm etc. the declaration was signed and verified by persons specified in Section 65 of the Finance Act, 1997.
7. Where voluntarily disclosed income was represented by jewellery, the value of the jewellery or bullion was substantiated by a registered valuer's certificate. In case the jewellery declared was from a period before the financial year 1987-88, the value for purposes of declaration was taken to be value as on April 1, 1987.
8. The disclosure made in respect of any assessment year did not affect the finality of any completed assessment.
9. The voluntarily disclosed income was not added to the total income of the declarant if the declarant credited such amount in his books of account and intimated the credit so made to the Assessing Officer.
10. VDIS did not apply to the following categories of persons: (a) those on whom an *order of detention* had been served under the Conservation of Foreign Exchange and Prevention of Smuggling Activities Act, 1974 in certain circumstances, (b) those punishable under the Narcotic

Drugs and Psychotropic Substances Act, 1985, (c) those punishable under the Terrorists and Disruptive Activities (Prevention) Act, 1987, (d) those notified under Section 3 of the Special Court (trial of offences relating to transaction in securities) Act, 1992, and (e) those on whom notices under Section 142 or 148 had been served.

11. A person was not eligible for the income disclosure benefit if that income was before or for a year when a search had been initiated under Section 132 or a requisition made under Section 132A. However, persons surveyed under Section 133A of the Income Tax Act were barred from making a declaration only for income in the year of the survey.
12. State Governments got 77.5 percent of the total resources secured under the scheme. The remaining portion, being share of the Central Government, was used entirely to finance the Basic Minimum Services Programme and infrastructure needs.

At a press conference on January 3, 1998, Finance Minister P. Chidambaran announced that VDIS netted ₹ 10,050 crore towards tax revenue. The total disclosure of black money in the six-month-long campaign was ₹ 33,000 crore and an estimated 4.6 lakh declarations were made under the VDIS.

6.3 Advance Tax Payment

Though the regular assessment in respect of any income is made in a later assessment year, the tax on such income is payable by way of advance payment or deduction at source. Section 208 of the Income Tax Act, 1961 makes it obligatory to pay advance tax in every case where the advance tax payable is ₹ 10,000 or more.

6.4 Withholding Tax [or Tax Deduction at Source (TDS)]

There are provisions under various sections of the Act regarding tax deduction at source (TDS) [3], e.g. deduction of tax from salaries (Section 192). Other incomes covered under the scheme of TDS include fees for professional or technical services, interest, rent from real estate, commission from insurance, sale of lottery tickets, and winnings from lotteries, crossword puzzles and horse racing.

In recent years, improvement in the percentage share of direct taxes (mainly income tax) has taken place due to widening of the tax base, presumptive taxation and broadening the scope of TDS. In this context, the Ninth Five Year Plan (1997-2002) observed, "The share of TDS in gross collection of income tax increased from about 23 percent in 1980-81 to about 37 percent in 1989-90, but declined subsequently to about 31 percent in 1994-95. One of the major loopholes which contributes to the decline in revenue from TDS relates to the branch-wise threshold of ₹ 10,000 for the purpose of deducting income tax at source from interest on time deposits with banks. Further, the provision for TDS does not apply to non-banking financial companies. Other deficiencies from which the TDS scheme suffers arise from lack of proper monitoring and scrutiny". [4]

6.5 Presumptive Tax for Small Traders [5]

In its Interim Report, submitted in December 1991, the Tax Reforms Committee examined the problems and possibilities of taxing the small business sector. The Committee suggested two new presumptive taxes on small businesses:

1. A fixed tax on businesses whose turnover was less than ₹ 5 lakh.
2. An estimated income scheme on small businesses with a turnover above ₹ 5 lakh but less than ₹ 25 lakh.

The schemes envisaged profit to be a certain percentage of turnover depending on the type of activity from which it was earned. The Government introduced the first scheme through the Finance Act, 1992, but deferred its decision to introduce the second scheme.

The presumptive tax system for persons engaged in retail trade with an annual turnover up to ₹ 5 lakh was introduced on an experimental basis. The scheme was in operation initially for two assessment years 1993-94 and 1994-95. It was continued after the expiry of these two years. The objective of the new simplified procedure for taxation was to widen the tax base by encouraging shopkeepers (including those engaged in vocations like tailoring, typewriting, photocopying, repair work etc.) and other small retail traders to pay taxes. The scheme had the following features:

1. The scheme was optional and open to individuals not assessed to tax earlier and who had an income from the business of retail trade having an annual turnover up to ₹ 5 lakh. The scheme was optional to avoid objection on constitutional grounds. If presumptive tax results in a higher tax burden than the one on the basis of book profit, it can be said to violate Article 14 of the Constitution which guarantees equality before law. Thus, the taxpayer had the option to pay presumptive tax or ask for regular assessment of his income, whichever he thought was advantageous to him.
2. Persons opting for the scheme were deemed to have a turnover of ₹ 5 lakh and their total income was deemed to be ₹ 35,000 (₹ 37,000 for A.Y. 1994-95) on which the tax worked out to ₹ 1,400 after allowing for the basic exemption of ₹ 28,000 (₹ 30,000 for A.Y. 1994-95).
3. A retail trader opting for the scheme had only to file the simplified statement (name, address, nature of business etc.) and pay a tax of ₹ 1,400 by 15th March of the financial year in which the income was earned.

Unfortunately, the scheme of presumptive taxation did not gain popularity with small traders and self-employed entrepreneurs. In 1992-93, the first year of the operation of the scheme, 1,16,644 persons opted for the scheme and paid a total tax of ₹ 16.4 crore, as against the anticipated revenue collection of ₹ 140 crore. [6] This was by no means a significant addition to the existing 70 lakh individual assessees under the income tax net. The number of shopkeepers and other small traders was much higher. The scheme touched only the tip of the iceberg.

The Government introduced through the Finance Act, 1994 two new schemes for estimating the income from the business of civil construction and plying or hiring trucks. The Finance Act, 1994 introduced Sections 44AD and 44AE in the Income Tax Act to provide for a method of estimating income from these businesses. While the section for civil construction applied to all assessees whose gross receipts from the business did not exceed ₹ 40 lakh, the section for plying trucks applied to businessmen owning not more than 10 trucks. Under Section 44AD, the income from these businesses was estimated at 8 percent of the gross receipts paid or payable to an assessee. Income of truck owners is assessed at ₹ 3,500 p.m. per heavy vehicle and at ₹ 3,150 p.m. per medium and light vehicle.

In the 1997-98 budget, the Finance Minister discontinued the presumptive scheme under Section 115K as it failed to yield the desired results. In its place, he introduced a new estimated income scheme for retail traders. The new scheme is applicable to persons engaged in the business of retail trade of any goods or merchandise having a total turnover of less than ₹ 40 lakh. The income of the trader will be estimated at 5 percent of the total turnover. A trader with a turnover of less than ₹ 10 lakh is exempted given the present exemption limit of ₹ 50,000. Assessees who file a return showing an income less than 5 per cent of turnover are required to maintain books of account and get their accounts audited.

6.5.1 Estimated Income Scheme for Small Businesses: This scheme, applicable for assessment year 2011-12 and onwards, applies to assessees engaged in any eligible business whose total turnover or gross receipts do not exceed ₹ 1 crore during a year. The scheme, under Section 44AD, is compulsory for all eligible assessees. Under the scheme, the income of an assessee from the eligible business is estimated at 8 percent of the total turnover in the previous year.

6.5.2 Estimated Income Scheme for Truck Owners: This scheme, provided under Section 44AE, applies to assesses engaged in business of plying, leasing or hiring trucks, owning not more than 10 trucks, at any time during the previous year. The income is estimated at ₹ 5,000 p.m. for each heavy goods vehicle and ₹ 4,500 p.m. for each vehicle other than heavy goods vehicle.

6.6 Permanent Account Number (PAN) or General Index Register Number (GIR)

In order to strengthen the efforts at enforcement, the Finance Minister in his 1998-99 budget made it obligatory for assessees to quote their PAN or GIR mandatorily in respect of the following high value transactions: purchase and sale of immovable property; purchase and sale of motor vehicles; transactions in shares exceeding ₹ 10 lakh; opening of new bank accounts; fixed deposits of more than ₹ 50,000; applications for allotment of telephone connections; and payments to hotels exceeding ₹ 25,000.

6.7 Survey of Income Tax

Income tax authorities may conduct, from time to time, a shop to shop or house to house survey to rope in new assessees. Potential assessees are required to fill up a questionnaire in Form 45-D. Officials conducting the survey cannot seize any books of account, cash, or articles. If any person fails to comply with a notice under section 133B requiring the survey information in Form 45-D, he is liable to pay a penalty up to ₹ 1,000 [Section 272AA].

6.8 Summons, and Search and Seizure

6.8.1 Summons: Under Section 131, an authorised income tax officer can issue summons when he has reasons to suspect that any income has been concealed by any person within his jurisdiction. Summons is issued to enforce attendance of any person for the purpose of examining him. The person concerned may be examined to verify the authenticity of various types of transactions, the following being the common ones.

A. Capital Contributions: Summons can be issued to owners of a business (i.e. proprietors, partners, and shareholders) to verify their capital contributions and sources of money thereof. Borrowed funds can be sources of money for capital contributions.

B. Business Transactions: An assessee makes claim in his return of income regarding purchases, sales, revenue expenditure, and capital outlays. To verify such claims, the assessing officer can issue summons to suppliers, buyers, and recipients of commissions, salaries, rent. etc.

C. Borrowing of Funds: An assessee may borrow funds from institutional and/or non-institutional sources for various purposes. Borrowings from non-institutional sources (e.g. private moneylenders, relatives, friends etc.) may need to be confirmed by income tax authorities. Hence, summons can be issued to persons who have lent money to explain sources of money lent.

D. Investment Transactions: Summons can be issued to any person who has made substantial investments in shares, securities, land, buildings, and costly consumer durables. The person so summoned is expected to explain with documentary evidence the sources of his funds. These sources may include borrowings, gifts received, property inherited, sale of jewellery etc. However, documentary evidence is necessary to prove these sources of money. It is advisable to reveal correct factual information which can be cross-verified.

6.8.2 Search and Seizure: To conduct search (popularly called raid) and seizure, an authorisation in the prescribed form is issued by the competent income tax authority under his signature and seal. Income tax officials are vested with considerable powers to carry out search operations. Thus, they can: (a) enter and search any building, place or vehicle in occupation of the person being searched, (b) break the lock and examine any box, locker, almirah etc., and (c) seize any books of account, other documents, money, bullion, jewellery etc. Books of account and other documents impounded cannot be retained beyond 180 days without obtaining approval of the Commissioner. However, the assessee can have copies made out of the original books impounded by the authorities [Sections 132 and 132A].

6.9 Penalties and Prosecutions

6.9.1 Penalties: Income Tax Act contains provisions under which penalties are imposed for various defaults committed by the taxpayers. The important provisions in this regard are summarised in Table 6.1.

Table 6.1: Select Penalty Provisions for Different Defaults under Income Tax Act, 1961

Section	Nature of default	Penalty
271(1)(C)	Concealment of particulars of income	Not less than the amount of tax sought to be evaded and not exceeding three times the amount of tax sought to be evaded
271A	Failure to keep or maintain books of account as required under Section 44AA	₹ 25,000
271C	Failure to deduct tax at source	Amount equal to tax which he failed to deduct or pay
271F	Failure to furnish return of income under Section 139(1) i.e. persons owning immovable property, motor vehicle, telephone etc.	₹ 5,000
272B	Failure to apply for allotment of permanent account number (PAN)	₹ 10,000

6.9.2 Prosecutions: Income Tax Act contains provisions under which prosecution proceedings can be started for different offences committed by taxpayers.

The important provisions in this regard are summarised in Table 6.2.

Table 6.2: Select Prosecution Provisions for Various Offences under Income Tax Act, 1961

Section	Nature of offence	Punishment
276B	Failure to deposit tax deducted at source or tax collected at source	Rigorous imprisonment up to 7 years (not less than 3 months) and fine
276C(2)	Wilful attempt to evade the payment of any tax, penalty or interest	Rigorous imprisonment up to 2 years (not less than 3 months) and fine
276CC	Wilful failure to furnish in due time return of income or return of fringe benefits	(a) Rigorous imprisonment up to 7 years (not less than 3 months) and fine if the amount sought to be evaded exceeds ₹ 25,00,000; (b) Imprisonment up to 2 years (not less than 3 months) and fine in other cases
277	Making a false statement in verification or delivering a false account	(a) Rigorous imprisonment up to 7 years (not less than 6 months) and fine if the amount sought to be evaded exceeds ₹ 25,00,000; (b) Rigorous imprisonment up to 2 years (not less than 3 months) and fine in other cases

6.9.3 Penal Provisions: A Comment: There are quite a few Sections in the Income Tax Act which confer discretionary powers on income tax officers. Thus, Section 273A of the Act allows income tax officers to reduce or waive penalties for tax evasion if it is voluntarily disclosed before being discovered by the assessing officer. According to the

Act, this can be done only once in the life time of a taxpayer. However, in practice it is likely that the penalty is waived several times for the same taxpayer even when the disclosure criterion is not met. The possibility of misuse of Section 273A cannot be ruled out.

Similarly, Section 273A (4) of the Act allows tax officers to reduce or waive penalty on grounds of genuine hardships.

Furthermore, under Section 279 (2) of the Act tax officers are empowered to compound an offence either before or after the institution of prosecution proceedings. These powers are discretionary and cannot be challenged in a court of law.

6.10 Use of Information Technology in Tax Administration

6.10.1 E-payment of Tax and E-filing of Returns: E-payment of tax is a facility provided to the taxpayers for making income tax payment through internet banking facility or through internet by using credit/debit cards. Assessees required to get their accounts audited under Section 44-AB and all companies are mandatorily required to make e-payment of tax.

While e-filing of returns through internet is mandatory for a company and a firm liable to audit under Section 44-AB, it is optional for other assessees. Similarly, it is mandatory for corporate deductors to furnish their TDS return in electronic form.

6.10.2 Digital Signature: A person desiring to furnish his return of income electronically, may sign it digitally or manually. For signing the return digitally, he is required to obtain a digital signature. A digital signature is the electronic signature issued by the certifying authority that shows the authenticity of the person signing the same.

6.11 Recent Legislative Measures to Prevent Generation of Black Money

A number of proactive steps have recently been taken in order to create an appropriate legislative framework for preventing the generation of black money and for its detection.

6.11.1 Prevention of Money Laundering Act (PMLA), 2002: PMLA was enacted to prevent money laundering and provide for confiscation of property derived from, or involved in, money laundering and for matters connected therewith or incidental thereto. The Act also addresses international obligations under the Political Declaration and Global Programme of Action adopted by the General Assembly of the United Nations to prevent money laundering.

To strengthen the provisions of the PMLA, amendments were carried out in 2009. These amendments have introduced new definitions to clarify and strengthen the Act and strengthened provisions related to attachment of property involved in money laundering and its seizure and confiscation. More offences have been added in Parts A and B of the Schedule to the Act, including those pertaining to insider trading and market manipulation as well as smuggling of antiques, terrorism funding, human trafficking other than prostitution, and a wider range of environmental crimes. A new category of offences with cross-border implications has been introduced as Part C.

The problem of black money is no longer restricted to the geo-political boundaries of any country. It has become a global menace that cannot be contained by any nation alone. In view of this, India has become a member of the Financial Action Task Force (FATF) [7] and Asia/Pacific Group on Money Laundering (APG) [8] which are committed to the effective implementation and enforcement of internationally accepted standards against money laundering and the financing of terrorism. Consequent to the submission of an action plan to the FATF for bringing India's anti-money-laundering legislation on par with international standards and to address some of the deficiencies of the Act that have been experienced by the implementing agencies, PMLA 2002 is further proposed to be amended through the Prevention of Money Laundering (Amendment) Bill, 2011, which is under consideration of the Parliament.

The Bill seeks to introduce the concept of *corresponding law* to link the provisions of Indian law with the laws of foreign countries and provide for transfer of the proceeds of the foreign predicate offence in any manner in India. It also proposes to enlarge the definition of the offence of money laundering to include therein activities like concealment, acquisition, possession, and use of proceeds of crime as criminal activities and remove the existing limit of ₹ 5 lakh for imposition of fine under the Act.

It also strengthens provisions for attachment and confiscation of the proceeds of crime and widens the investigative powers of the concerned officials and clubs offences listed under Schedules A and B into a single Schedule.

6.11.2 Benami Transaction (Prohibition) Bill, 2011: This comprehensive legislation was introduced in the Lok Sabha on August 18, 2011 and is currently being examined by the Standing Committee on Finance. It will iron out the infirmities in the Benami Transaction (Prohibition) Act enacted in 1988 and formalise the procedure for implementing the benami law, including the procedure for determination, confiscation, prosecution, and miscellaneous requirements.

This Bill defines benami property and a benami transaction in terms of a transaction or agreement where a property is transferred to or held by a person for a consideration provided or paid by another person. Such a property is held for the immediate or future benefit, direct or indirect, of the person providing the consideration. A transaction or arrangement in respect of a property carried out or made in a fictitious name or where the owner of the property is not aware of or denies knowledge of such ownership is also included in the definition of benami transaction. The Bill specifies the consequences of benami transactions in the form of confiscation of the benami property and imprisonment up to 2 years in addition to a fine. This Bill also provides the procedure for enquiry and determination of benami property and its consequences as well as the authorities empowered to act for this purpose, including the appellate authorities. After the report of the Standing Committee is received, the Benami Transactions (Prohibition) Bill, 2011 will be moved for passage in Parliament and the relevant rules notified thereafter.

6.11.3 Public Procurement Bill, 2012: The Public Procurement Bill, 2012 was approved by the Union Cabinet on April 12, 2012 for introduction in Parliament. The Bill seeks to regulate procurement by ministries/departments of the Central Government and its attached/subordinate offices, Central public sector enterprises (CPSEs), autonomous and statutory bodies controlled by the Central Government and other procuring entities with the objectives of ensuring transparency, accountability and probity in the procurement process, fair and equitable treatment of bidders, promoting competition, enhancing efficiency and economy, safeguarding integrity in the procurement process, and enhancing public confidence in public procurement.

The Bill is based on broad principles and envisages a set of detailed rules, guidelines, and model documents. It builds on national and international experience and best practices as appropriate for the needs of the Government of India. It will create a statutory framework for public procurement which will provide greater accountability, transparency, and enforceability of the regulatory framework. The Bill codifies the essential principles governing procurement required for achieving economy, efficiency, and quality as well as combating corruption. It legally obligates procuring entities and their officials to comply with these principles. It also ensures that competition will be maximised in procurement, while providing for adequate flexibility for different types of procurement needs. It puts in place a strong framework of transparency and accountability through a public procurement portal and a grievance redressal system in which an independent mechanism, chaired by a retired High Court Judge, will review grievances.

6.11.4 Prevention of Bribery of Foreign Public Officials and Officials of the Public International Organisations Bill, 2011: This Bill was introduced in the Lok Sabha on March 25, 2011 and is under consideration of the Standing Committee. The Bill seeks to prevent corruption relating to bribery of foreign public officials and officials of public international organisations and to address matters connected therewith or incidental thereto. The proposed legislation prohibits acceptance of gratification by foreign public officials or officials of public international organisations as well as the act of giving such gratification or its abetment. The Bill also empowers the Central Government to enter into agreements with foreign countries for enforcing the provisions, makes offences under the proposed act extraditable, and provides for attachment, seizure and confiscation of property in India or the respective country and mutual assistance in this regard.

6.11.5 Lokpal and Lokayukta Bill, 2011: After being passed by the Lok Sabha, it is now under consideration of the Rajya Sabha. It provides for the establishment of the institution of Lokpal to inquire into allegations of corruption against certain public functionaries and for matters connected therewith or incidental thereto. The Bill envisages setting up of the institution of Lokpal consisting of a chairperson and 8 members with the stipulation that half of the members shall be judicial members. It shall have its own Investigation Wing and Prosecution Wing with such officers and staff as are necessary to carry out its functions. The Lokpal shall inquire into allegations of corruption made in respect of the following:

- Prime Minister after he has demitted office.
- A Minister of the Union.
- A Member of Parliament.
- Any Group 'A' officer or equivalent.
- Chairperson or member or officer equivalent to Group 'A' in any body/board/corporation/authority/company/society/trust/autonomous body established by an Act of Parliament or wholly or partly financed or controlled by the Central

Government.

- Any director, manager, secretary or other officer of a society or association of persons or trust wholly or partly financed or aided by the government or in receipt of any donations from the public and whose annual income exceeds such amount as the Central Government may by notification specify.

However, organisations created for religious purposes and receiving public donations shall be outside the purview of the Lokpal. The Lokpal shall not require sanction or approval under Section 197 of the Code of Criminal Procedure, 1973 or Section 19 of the Prevention of Corruption Act, 1988 in cases where prosecution is proposed. The Lokpal shall also have powers to attach the property of corrupt public servants acquired through corrupt means.

6.11.6 Citizens' Grievance Redressal Bill: The Right of Citizens for Time Bound Delivery of Goods and Services and Redressal of their Grievances Bill, 2011, which is presently under consideration of the Lok Sabha outlines the responsibilities of government departments towards citizens and how someone who is denied the service due to him can seek redressal. It mandates that every public authority or government department has to publish a citizen's charter listing all services rendered by that department along with a grievance redressal mechanism for non-compliance with the citizen's charter. It also sets up a Central Public Grievances Redressal Commission, with an equivalent in every state, and provides for a designated authority from a department other than the one against which the complaint has been filed to address the complaint. The other features of the Bill are as under:

1. The Citizen's charter has to clearly explain the complaint redressal system for that office, like which officer in that department the complaint should be registered with.
2. Every government department or public authority shall create an *information and facilitation centre* that could include a customer helpline or help desk to deliver services

and handle complaints.

3. Every public authority will appoint or designate grievance redressal officers whose contact information will be clearly shared with the public. The grievance redressal officer shall provide the public with all necessary assistance in filing complaints. Within two days of the complaint being registered, the citizen who has filed a complaint will receive—by SMS or mail—a unique complaint number and a time frame within which the complaint will be handled. That time frame cannot exceed 30 days from when the complaint was received.
4. The grievance redressal officer has to ensure that the person who made the complaint is informed in writing with an action taken report on how his/her complaint was handled. If this does not happen, the citizen can appeal to a designated authority. This officer can summon others and ask them to testify under oath.
5. The designated authority has to ensure that the appeal is acted upon within 30 days. It can fine the officer concerned and compensate the citizen, if appropriate.
6. If a citizen is not happy with the designated authority's response or decision, he can take his complaint to the State Public Grievance Redressal Commission (assuming that the complaint is against a government department that is under the jurisdiction of a state government). Each state shall set up this body. It will have a chief commissioner and a maximum of ten other commissioners. They will be appointed by a committee consisting of the chief minister, the leader of opposition in that state, and a sitting judge of the High Court. The commissioners will have a term of five years.
7. For citizens who are unhappy with a service provided to them from a government office that is under the jurisdiction of the Central Government, they can finally appeal to the Central Public Grievance Redressal Commission. This body will have a chief commissioner

and a maximum of ten commissioners who will be appointed by the President after they are chosen by a committee comprising the Prime Minister, the leader of opposition, and a sitting judge of the Supreme Court.
8. If citizens are unhappy with the decision of the Central or State Commissions, they can appeal to the Lokayukta or Lokpal.

6.11.7 Judicial Standards and Accountability Bill, 2010: It was passed by the Lok Sabha and is under consideration of the Rajya Sabha. The Bill provides a mechanism for enquiring into complaints against judges of the Supreme Court and High Courts, lays down judicial standards, and requires judges of the Supreme Court and High Courts to declare their assets and liabilities. The Bill seeks to replace the Judges (Inquiry) Act, 1968 while retaining its basic features. The enactment of the Bill will address the growing concerns regarding the need to ensure greater accountability of the higher judiciary by bringing in more transparency and will further strengthen the credibility and independence of the judiciary. The Bill seeks to lay down enforceable standards of conduct for judges. The main features of the Bill are as under:

1. It requires judges to declare their assets, lays down judicial standards, and establishes processes for removal of judges of the Supreme Court and High Courts.
2. It requires judges to declare their assets and liabilities and also those of their spouses and children.
3. The Bill establishes the National Judicial Oversight Committee, the Complaints Scrutiny Panel, and an investigation committee. Any person can make a complaint against a judge to the Oversight Committee on grounds of *misbehaviour*.
4. A motion for removal of a judge on grounds of misbehaviour can also be moved in Parliament. Such a motion will be referred for further inquiry to the Oversight Committee.
5. Complaints and inquiries against judges will be

confidential and frivolous complaints will be penalised.

6. The Oversight Committee may issue advisories or warnings to judges and also recommend their removal to the President.

6.11.8 Public Interest Disclosure and Protection to Persons Making the Disclosure Bill, 2010: Commonly known as the Whistleblowers' Bill, it was passed by the Lok Sabha and is under consideration of the Rajya Sabha. The Bill seeks to provide *adequate protection to persons reporting corruption or wilful misuse of discretion which causes demonstrable loss to the government or commission of a criminal offence by a public servant*. While the measure sets out the procedure to inquire into disclosures and provides adequate safeguards against victimisation of the whistleblower, it also seeks to provide punishment for false or frivolous complaints.

6.11.9 Electronic Delivery of Services Bill, 2011: It seeks to provide for electronic delivery of public services by the Government to all persons to ensure transparency, efficiency, accountability, accessibility and reliability in delivery of such services. It was tabled before the Parliament in December 2011.

End Notes

1. Government of India, Ministry of Finance, *Final Report of Direct Taxes Enquiry Committee* (Chairman: Justice K.N. Wanchoo), 1971, para 2.52.
2. Government of India, Ministry of Finance, *Report of the Direct Taxes Administration Enquiry Committee* (Chairman: Mahavir Tyagi), 1958-59, p. 149.
3. TDS is a system of collecting income tax whereby money is periodically deducted by the employers, financial institutions, and others from wages of employees, returns on securities, and other payments. Thus, intermediaries (or third parties) do the job on behalf of the government as regards assessment of the taxable base and the collection of tax thereon.

   Generally, a fixed percentage is withheld from the payment made and the same is deposited in government's account. At the time of filing the return of income, the taxpayer encloses withholding tax receipts and in case of overpayment he can claim refund of tax.

Tax withholding system (also called tax deduction at source or Pay-As-You-Earn) satisfies the canon of convenience both for the fiscal authorities and the taxpayers. It is beneficial for the government because it reduces the possibility of tax evasion, ensures prompt tax payment, and simplifies tax collection. It does not allow any lag between the time of receiving income and the time of tax payment. For the taxpayer, it is an instalment plan of taxation and hence convenient.

However, tax withholding involves additional paper work on the part of tax deductors. It also adds to the burden of taxpayers who have to obtain tax deduction certificates from deductors, fill additional tax forms, and wait for refunds.

4. Government of India, Planning Commission, *Ninth Five Year Plan* (1997-2002), Volume I, p. 168.
5. **Presumptive Tax:** In every country, there are some soft-to-tax and hard-to-tax sources of income. Wages and salaries are properly recorded and therefore it is easy to assess and collect taxes on them through the Pay-As-You-Earn (PAYE) system. Similarly, income from securities paid through banks can easily be subjected to deduction at source.

   Contrarily, the three hard-to-tax classes of the non-corporate sector are: (a) unincorporated commercial and industrial units, (b) self-employed professionals, and (c) rich peasantry. The problem of taxing the first two categories relates to accounting difficulties while in the case of third category, it is essentially the lack of political will. Non-reporting and under-reporting of income is quite sizeable in these sectors. The growing small business sector is a tax haven. It is very difficult to enforce a reliable system of book-keeping to assess earnings of this sector. Pragmatically, a system of lump sum taxation may be tried in place of taxation of profits.

   Presumptive tax relates to the use of appropriate indicators of income, wealth etc. instead of the actual records of these tax bases. In the case of income tax, a presumptive tax is imposed on the basis of an estimated taxable income. Presumptive income is exogenously determined. The base for the presumptive income tax is fixed and does not depend on the behaviour of individual entrepreneurs. In essence, a presumptive income tax works like a lump sum tax and therefore does not impose marginal tax burden on actual income. Varying methods of presumptive taxation are in operation in Israel, Argentina, Chile, and Columbia. The French *forfait* system is a typical example of presumptive taxation. The chief advantage of presumptive taxation is its simplicity, both for the tax collectors and the taxpayers. It is, therefore, cost-effective for the administration. The simplicity attribute may also encourage tax compliance. Presumptive taxation particularly suits the developing countries with a large unorganised business sector consisting of small retail establishments, and self-employed professionals. It is easy to administer this tax which can become an effective source of revenue. It also promotes horizontal equity.

The French *forfait* system has several features. Firstly, the taxable profit of a given business unit is agreed upon mutually between the tax authorities and the assessee. Secondly, the assessment remains valid for a limited number of years. Finally, the taxpayer is required to submit a set of simple facts to the authorities, namely the amount of his purchases and sales, the wage bill, the value of his inventory, and the number of employees. Alternatively, small businesses may be subject to a system of licence fee charged in accordance with some well-defined criteria such as the location of business and its size.

6. Government of India, *Economic Survey*, 1993-94, p. 26.
7. See section 1.5.6 of Chapter 1 of this book.
8. See section 1.5.7 of Chapter 1 of this book.

7

International Aspects of Indian Taxation (Double Taxation)

Business and investment operations of individuals and companies are becoming increasingly international in scope in the wake of current wave of globalisation and openness sweeping across the countries of the world. Tax systems of different countries differ in terms of types of taxes, definition of income and expenses, exemptions and concessions, rates and collection procedures. Varying tax practices of different countries complicate decision-making by multinational enterprises as to what is most profitable on an international basis. The study of international taxation becomes relevant in this context.

7.1 What is Double Taxation?

Double taxation (or tax duplication) occurs when the same base (e.g. income) is assessed twice, either by the same tax jurisdiction or by two competing tax jurisdictions, either at different levels of government in a country or at the same level of government in different countries. All the three versions of double taxation are described below.

7.1.1 Double Taxation by the Same Tax Jurisdiction: A common example of this kind of double taxation is the taxation of corporate earnings, first in the form of corporate income tax, and then in the form of personal income tax on dividends distributed to shareholders. Tax laws usually contain provisions which mitigate or even eliminate tax duplication of this kind. Under one method, a shareholder is granted credit against his tax liability on overall income for the tax paid by the company on distributed profits. The credit may be granted on full or partial basis (say 50 percent) on account of company tax on distributed profits.

7.1.2 Double Taxation by Competing Tax Jurisdictions at Different Levels of Government in a Country: Double taxation of this type arises when different levels of government impose taxes on the same base, e.g. taxation of income by Federal and State Governments in USA, and Canada. This kind of double taxation arises due to joint occupancy of tax fields. [1]

7.1.3 Double Taxation by Competing Tax Jurisdictions at Same Level of Government in Different Countries: This kind of double taxation is also called *international double taxation* or *territorial multiple taxation.* In this case, two sovereign countries claim jurisdiction in taxing the same base, usually income.

7.2 International Double Taxation

International double taxation occurs when a taxpayer is resident in one country but has a source of income situated in another country so that tax is imposed by both the countries on the same income. Thus, international double taxation arises due to overlapping of two tax claims of two or more countries. OECD has defined international double taxation as, "the imposition of comparable taxes in two (or more) states on the same taxpayer in respect of the same subject matter for identical periods". [2]

In most cases, individuals work in countries where they live and companies invest in countries in which they are resident. However, world economies are becoming increasingly international and flow of labour and capital from one country to another is common. Multinationals operate in a number of countries, and individual investors possess internationally diversified investment portfolios. Thus, companies and individuals receive foreign income in the form of profits, dividends and royalties. When a person undertakes cross-border activities or maintains connections in two or more countries, he is likely to encounter the tax laws of another country. That encounter influences the way in which the person is taxed in his home country. This is how the tax systems of different countries get linked with each other.

Like international law, there is no such thing as international taxation. Taxes are not international because they are not levied at an international level by any supranational authority. Taxes are levied by central, state and local governments. International taxation (or more appropriately international tax law) includes all those rules which affect the taxation of a person and which are different from the rules that would apply if all his activities and connections were in a single country. These rules include the laws, regulations, juridical pronouncements and practices of different countries. They are meant to minimise/eliminate international tax duplication so that international flow of labour and capital is not unduly obstructed.

7.3 Assignment Rules of Foreign Income

Two fundamental assignment rules govern the right of nations to impose taxes on foreign income: (a) the source rule or the territoriality rule, and (b) the residence or domicile rule.

7.3.1 Source Rule: The source rule holds that income ought to be taxed in the country in which it originates irrespective of whether the income accrues to a resident or a non-resident assessee. The claim for tax jurisdiction is made on the ground that source country allows non-residents to use its infrastructure and other inputs for production purposes and therefore it can legitimately take a bite into their earnings.

7.3.2 Residence Rule: According to the residence rule, the power to tax foreign income should belong to the country in which the taxpayer resides. The claim of the residence (or home) country rests on the ground that the source (or host) country utilises and benefits from manpower and other resources trained and perfected by the home country. The tests of residence including nationality of individual assessees are complex and vary from country to country. Similarly, different countries follow different rules to define a domestic/foreign company.

7.4 Methods to Alleviate International Double Taxation

The problem of international tax duplication can be avoided if all the countries follow either the source or the residence rule. In practice, most countries exercise source and residence rules concurrently. If a country observes only the residence rule, then it surrenders tax claim on incomes which originate within its political jurisdiction and accrue to non-residents. A country would normally not go for this option which favours the foreigners vis-à-vis its own citizens. In most cases, countries tax their residents on their world income, and the non-residents on their incomes originating within their borders. International tax duplication arises when the country of residence extends the tax net to the world income of a taxpayer and the host country follows the source rule. Double taxation of this kind discourages international movement of factors of production.

Various methods may be followed by concerned countries to reduce or even eliminate double taxation of foreign-source income of their residents.

7.4.1 Exemption Method: A country may voluntarily and unilaterally sacrifice its tax claim on the foreign income of its residents. In other words, foreign income of residents is exempt from taxation in the home country. For example, there is no further tax on repatriated profits in countries such as France and Germany.

7.4.2 Foreign Tax Credit: The home country permits deduction of taxes paid by the residents in the host country (on dividends, royalties etc.) from the tax on world-wide income due in the home country. The foreign tax credit is a mechanism provided unilaterally by a number of countries to alleviate the effect of double taxation. The object is to reduce tax on foreign-source income to the extent that income has already been taxed in the foreign jurisdiction. Under the tax credit system, the taxpayer pays the higher of the two taxes. If the foreign tax is the same or higher than the domestic tax, then the tax credit reduces the domestic tax liability on the foreign income to nil.

A foreign tax credit system was introduced in Australia on July 1, 1987. Under this system, the foreign-source income of residents is taxed at normal rates in Australia, with a credit granted for the foreign taxes paid. Other important countries which operate a tax credit mechanism as a means of eliminating double taxation are USA, UK, Canada, and Japan.

A. Tax Sparing Credit: Developing countries often give tax incentives, e.g. tax holiday to encourage foreign investments. Many developed countries provide, in their double tax treaties with developing countries, for a tax sparing credit. Under tax sparing, the investor is deemed to have paid the tax foregone in the country of source (say, India) so that the investor's country of residence (say, USA) grants a tax credit for the tax not charged by the source country. In other words, the residence country treats the income remitted as if it had been fully taxed and had not benefited from the tax incentives (of the host country). This ensures that the full benefit of the tax incentive goes to the investor and is not simply transferred to the residence country's treasury.

7.4.3 Bilateral Tax Treaties: International double taxation is also avoided through bilateral tax treaties (or double tax treaties). A double tax treaty is a convention or an agreement among countries for the avoidance of double taxation of income and capital and bringing uniformity in the allocation of taxation rights in cross-border situations. It is essentially a bargain between two treaty countries as regards the division of tax revenue between them in respect of income falling to be taxed in both jurisdictions. Since treaty negotiations involve bargaining, each side seeks concessions from the other and it is not necessary that strict *quid pro quo* is achieved in the end.

Apart from relieving double taxation, a double tax treaty aids commercial relations between treaty partners. It creates an environment of fiscal certainty which encourages trade and investment between countries. It provides rules for resolving problems of dual residence or dual source of income, defines the different forms of taxable income, and determines the taxing rights of the two treaty countries. An important provision of all double tax treaties is the machinery for administrative co-operation between the tax authorities of treaty partners.

The advantages and disadvantages of a double tax treaty depend on the flow of trade and investment between treaty partners. If these flows are in balance, which is a rarity, the benefits and costs would be truly reciprocal. Where the flows of trade and investment are unbalanced, the advantages of the treaty may be weighed more in favour of one treaty partner than the other, though the provisions of the treaty may be expressed in reciprocal terms. This is generally the case regarding tax treaties between developed and underdeveloped countries where flows of trade and investment are one-sided.

Most tax treaties are bilateral. Some international organisations have done commendable work in the development and harmonisation of bilateral double tax conventions. Model tax treaties drawn up by these organisations have helped to harmonise national approaches to double tax relief. They have facilitated the negotiation of tax treaties by eliminating the need for elaborate analysis and protracted discussion of every issue involved in each treaty.

In 1963, OECD published a Draft Double Taxation Convention. In 1977, it issued a Model Double Taxation Convention based on the experience of OECD member states since 1963. The OECD Model gives the primary right of taxation to the state of residence. It operates largely in favour of the developed capital exporting countries, and to the consequent detriment of underdeveloped countries which are net importers of foreign investment.

In 1966, OECD issued a draft convention on estates and inheritances. In 1982, it published a revised version of the same which included gifts also. The OECD conventions have been widely accepted among OECD member states and other developed countries.

The United Nations adopted a resolution in 1967 to constitute a group of experts on tax treaties between developed and developing countries. Special problems arise where a double tax treaty is concluded between developed and developing countries. Based on the report of the group of experts, the United Nations issued in 1979 a manual for tax treaty negotiators. In 1980, it issued its Model Double Taxation Convention between developed and developing countries.

The basic difference between the United Nations model and the OECD model is that the former predominantly gives the source country the right to tax income while the latter grants the country of residence the right to tax income. The United Nations model is generally used when one of the countries is a developing one. This is so because normally investments flow from a developed country to a developing country which *ipso facto* means that incomes flow from developing to developed countries, i.e. developing countries are the source of income.

7.4.4 Multilateral Tax Treaties: Multilateral double tax treaties, though considered at different times in various contexts, have not gained acceptance for being complex. It is difficult to understand and apply a multilateral treaty than a bilateral one. Moreover, a multilateral convention is less flexible in terms of amendment, revision, or termination.

Though multilateral approach is not generally followed, there are, at least, three notable multilateral double income tax agreements.

1. **Andean Pact:** This agreement among the member states of Andean Group (Bolivia, Chile, Columbia, Ecuador, Peru, and Venezuela) is based on the principle of giving the state of source the exclusive right of taxation.
2. **Comecon Conventions:** There are two multilateral agreements for the avoidance of double taxation among 8 of

the 10 member states of Comecon (Bulgaria, Czechoslovakia, erstwhile GDR, Hungary, Mongolia, Poland, Romania, erstwhile U.S.S.R, Cuba, and Vietnam). The last two are not signatories to the multilateral agreements.

3. **Nordic Countries:** A multilateral treaty covering tax on income and capital exists among Nordic countries (Denmark, Finland, Iceland, Norway, and Sweden).

7.5 Indian Law on Double Tax Relief

As in most other countries, India gives unilateral as well as treaty relief in respect of foreign taxes suffered by Indian residents on their foreign income. Sections 90 and 91 of the Income Tax Act, 1961 deal with relief from international double taxation. Section 90 is for taxpayers who have paid the tax to a country with which India has signed a DTAA, while Section 91 provides relief to taxpayers who have paid tax to a country with which India has not signed a DTAA.

Section 90 of the Act gives relief bilaterally through tax treaties. It provides, *inter alia*, that a treaty may be entered into: (a) for grant of relief in respect of income which is taxed in both the countries, (b) for the avoidance of double taxation on income, (c) for exchange of information for the prevention of evasion or avoidance of income tax, and (d) for the recovery of income tax.

Broadly speaking, India's tax treaties contain two alternatives: (i) Income which arises in the territory of one of the contracting States is not taxed by the other contracting State (exclusion method). (ii) Income is taxed in both the countries in accordance with their respective tax laws but the country of the residence of the taxpayer allows him a credit against the tax charged thereon in the country of the source of such income (tax credit method). Where any such agreement for avoidance of double taxation exists, the provisions of the Act applies to the extent they are more beneficial to the assessee.

Section 91 grants unilateral relief from double taxation to

the residents in respect of foreign tax paid abroad. It is noteworthy that Section 91 comes into force only when relief is not available under Section 90. Following are the requirements of Section 91: (a) the assessee should be a resident of India in the previous year, (b) such income should not be deemed to accrue in India under the provisions of the Act, (c) the income should be taxed in both the countries and there is no double tax treaty with that country, and (d) the assessee should have in fact paid the tax in such foreign country either by deduction or otherwise.

Thus, if an Indian resident proves that tax has been paid in respect of his income which accrued or arose to him in the countries with which India has no agreement for double taxation relief, he is entitled to a deduction from the Indian income tax payable by him.

7.6 Salient Features of a Typical Tax Treaty between India and another Country

India has entered into tax treaties with 83 countries. This means that there are agreed rates of tax and jurisdictions on specified types of income arising in a country to a tax resident of another country.

7.6.1 Scope of the Treaty: A typical tax treaty between India and another country covers only residents of India and the other contracting country who have entered into the agreement with India. Such agreement generally provides that the laws of the two contracting states will govern the taxation of income in respective states except when express provision to the contrary is made in the agreement.

Chapter I (Articles 1 and 2) of a typical tax treaty contain the personal scope of the tax treaty and the taxes covered under the treaty. Chapter II (Articles 3 and 4) deal with general definitions. For instance, Article 3 generally deals with definitions of the terms like State, tax, person, company, enterprise, international traffic, nationals, competent authority etc. Article 4 defines the term "resident" for the purpose of a given tax treaty. Normally, the term "resident of one of the States" means any person who, under the laws of that State, is liable to tax therein by reason of his domicile, residence, place of management or any other criterion of a similar nature.

A situation may arise when originally the tax provision in the other contracting state gave concessional treatment compared to India at a particular time but Indian laws were subsequently amended to bring incidence of tax to a level lower than the tax rate existing in the other contracting state. Since the tax treaties are meant to be beneficial and not intended to put taxpayers of a contracting state to a disadvantage, Section 90 of the Income Tax Act, 1961 specifies that where the Government of India has entered into a Double Taxation Avoidance Agreement with other countries, then the provision of the relevant DTAA or the Income Tax Act, 1961 whichever is more beneficial to the assessee, shall be applicable.

7.6.2 Permanent Establishment: Article 5 of the tax treaties entered into by India with different countries defines the term "permanent establishment" as fixed place of business through which the business of an enterprise is wholly or partly carried on. More specifically, the term "permanent establishment" includes: (a) a place of management, (b) a branch, (c) an office, (d) a factory, (e) a workshop, (f) a mine, an oil or gas well, a quarry or any other place of extraction of natural resources, (g) a warehouse, in relation to a person providing storage facilities for others, (h) a farm, plantation or other place where agriculture, forestry, plantation or related activities are carried on, (i) a store or premises used as a sales outlet, (j) an installation or structure used for the exploration or exploitation of natural resources, and (k) a building site or construction, installation or assembly project or supervisory activities in connection therewith.

A comparative study of articles on permanent establishment in respect of certain selected tax treaties reveals that there is no uniformity or consistency in defining the existence of a permanent establishment based on the minimum threshold period of existence.

7.6.3 Provisions for Taxation under the Tax Treaty: Chapter III of India's tax treaties deals with taxation of income including income from immovable property, business profits, dividends, interest, royalty, technical fees and the like.

A. Income from Immovable Property (Article 6): Article 6 provides that income derived by a resident of one of the States from immovable property situated in the other State may be taxed in that other State.

B. Business Profits (Article 7): Imposition of tax on a foreign enterprise is done only if it has a permanent establishment in the contracting state. Tax is computed by treating the permanent establishment as a distinct and independent enterprise.

In determining the profits of a permanent establishment, most tax treaties allow as deduction, expenses which are incurred for the purposes of the business of the permanent establishment, including executive and general administrative expenses.

The UN Model Convention (generally followed by India), *inter alia*, states that in the determination of profits of a permanent establishment, no deduction shall be allowed for amounts paid (otherwise than towards reimbursement of actual expenses) by the permanent establishment to the head office of the enterprise or any of its other offices, by way of royalties, fees or other similar payments in return for the use of patents or other rights, or by way of commission, for specific services performed. In this respect, it is interesting to note that except in respect of tax treaties with a few countries, the above provision of UN Model Convention has not been considered in many of the treaties. This implies that in respect of most of the tax treaties, expenditure incurred by the permanent establishment towards royalties, fees for technical services etc. would become an allowable expenditure, thereby reducing the taxable income leading to loss of revenue.

Further, most tax treaties provide that no profits shall be

attributed to a permanent establishment by reason of the mere purchase by that permanent establishment of goods or merchandise for the enterprise. The profits to be attributed to the permanent establishment shall be determined by the same method year by year unless there is good and sufficient reason to the contrary.

C. Income from Air and Shipping Transport (Articles 8 and 8A): Income derived from the operation of air transport in international traffic by an enterprise of one contracting state will not be taxed in the other contracting state. In respect of an enterprise of one contracting state, income earned in the other contracting state from the operation of ships in international traffic, will be taxed in that contracting state wherein the place of effective management of enterprise is situated. However, some treaties contain provisions to tax the income in the other contracting state also, although at reduced rate. These provisions do not apply to coastal traffic.

D. Associated Enterprises (Article 9): In order to plug loop holes for tax evasion, Article 9 in tax treaties provides for taxing the notional income in case of associated enterprises. Where an enterprise of a Contracting State participates directly or indirectly in the management, control or capital of an enterprise of the other Contracting State and conditions are made or imposed between the two enterprises in their commercial or financial relations which differ from those which would be made between independent enterprises, then any profits which would, but for those conditions, have accrued to one of the enterprises, but, by the reason of those conditions, have not so accrued, may be included in the profits of that enterprise and taxed accordingly.

E. Dividends (Article 10): India generally follows the UN Model for taxation of various sources of income like dividends, interest, royalty and technical fees. Rates of tax, which may be withheld from dividends, interest, royalty are to be negotiated bilaterally, unlike the OECD Model which specifies thee maximum rate. However, where a tax treaty provides for a particular mode of computation of income, the same shall be followed irrespective of the provisions of the Income Tax Act.

Dividends paid by a Company which is a resident of a Contracting State to a resident of the other Contracting State will be taxed in both the States. Where a company which is a resident of a Contracting State derives profits or income from the other Contracting State, that other State may not impose any tax on dividends paid by the company, except insofar as such dividends are paid to be a resident of that other State or insofar as the holding in respect of which the dividends are paid is effectively connected with a permanent establishment or a fixed base situated in that other State.

F. Interest (Article 11): Interest paid in a Contracting State to resident of the other Contracting State is chargeable to tax in both the States. This, however, shall not apply if the beneficial owner of the interest, being a resident of a Contracting State, carries on business in the other Contracting State in which the interest arises, through a permanent establishment situated therein, or performs in that other Contracting State independent personal services from a fixed base situated therein, and the debt-claim in respect of which the interest is paid is effectively connected with such permanent establishment or fixed base. In such case the provisions of Article 7 or Article 14, as the case may be, shall apply.

G. Royalties, Fees for Technical Services (Article 12): Generally, royalties, fees for technical services and payments for the use of equipment arising in one of the States and paid to a resident of the other State is taxed in both the States. The term "royalties" is normally defined as payments of any kind received as a consideration for the use of, or the right to use, any copyright of literary, artistic or scientific work, including cinematograph films, or films or tapes used for radio or television broadcasting, any patent, trade mark, design or model, plan, secret formula or process, or for the use of, or the right to use, industrial, commercial, or scientific equipment, or for information concerning industrial, commercial or scientific experience but does not include any payments in respect of the operation of mineral deposits, sources and other natural resources. The term "fees for technical services" is usually defined as payments of any kind to any person, other than payments to an employee of the person making the payments and to any individual for independent personal services, in consideration for services of a managerial, technical or consultative nature. Those tax treaties which have provisions for taxation of "payments for the use of equipment" define it as payments of any kind received as a consideration for the use of, or the right to use industrial, commercial or scientific equipment.

It is noteworthy that while some tax treaties have provisions for taxation of royalties, fees for technical services and payments for use of equipment, some others only have provisions for royalties.

Some Double Taxation Avoidance agreements provide that income by way of interest, royalty or fee for technical services is charged to tax on net basis. This may result in tax deducted at source from sums paid to non-residents which may be more than the final tax liability. The assessing officer has therefore been empowered under Section 195 to determine the appropriate proportion of the amount from which tax is to be deducted at source. There are instances where as per the Income Tax Act, tax is required to be deducted at a rate prescribed in tax treaty. However this may require foreign companies to apply for refund. To obviate such difficulties Section 2(37A) provides that tax may be deducted at source at the rate applicable in a particular case as per Section 195 on the sums payable to non-residents or in accordance with the rates specified in DTAAs.

Section 195 specifies the withholding tax rates for various categories of income. Tax is deductible at source under Section 195 at these specified rates or rates specified in double taxation avoidance agreements entered into by the Central Government under Section 90, whichever is lower.

H. Capital Gains: Capital gains will be taxed in the state where the capital asset is situated at the time of sale. More specifically, gains derived by a resident of a contracting state from the alienation of immovable property situated in the other contracting state may be taxed in that other State. Similarly, gains from the alienation of movable property forming part of the business property of a permanent establishment which an enterprise of a contracting state has in the other contracting state may be taxed in that other State. Gains from the alienation of any property other than those mentioned above shall normally be taxable only in the contracting state of which the alienator is a resident.

I. Independent Personal Services: Income derived by an individual who is a resident of a Contracting State from the performance of professional services or other independent activities of a similar character shall be taxable only in that State. However, if he has a fixed base regularly available to him in the other contracting state for the purpose of performing his activities, the income may be taxed in the other contracting state but only so much of it as is attributable to that fixed base. (The term professional services include especially, independent scientific, literary, artistic, educational or teaching activities as well as the independent activities of physicians, surgeons, lawyers, engineers, architects, dentists and accountants).

J. Dependent Personal Services: Salaries, wages and other similar remuneration derived by a resident of a contracting state in respect of an employment shall be taxable only in that State unless the employment is exercised, in the other contracting state. If the employment is so exercised, such remuneration as is derived therefrom may be taxed in that other State. Most of the tax treaties provide that where the recipient is present in the source country for a period not exceeding 183 days in the concerned year and remuneration is paid by an employer who is not a resident of the source country, then remuneration so received shall be taxable only in the country of residence of the recipient.

K. Directors Fees: Directors fees and similar payments derived by a resident of one of the contracting states as a member of the board of directors of a company which is a resident of the other contracting state may be taxed in that other State.

L. Entertainers: Income derived by residents of one of the contracting states as entertainers, such as theatre, motion picture, radio or television artists, musicians and athletes, from their personal activities as such exercised in the other contracting state, may be taxed in that other State.

M. Pensions and Annuities: Pensions and annuities paid to a resident of one of the contracting states shall be taxable only in that State.

N. Government Service: Remuneration, other than a pension or annuity, paid by one of the contracting states or political sub-division or local authority of that State to any individual in respect of services rendered in the discharge of governmental functions shall be taxable only in that State. However, such remuneration shall be taxable only in the other contracting state if the services are rendered in that other State and the recipient is a resident of that other State.

O. Professors and Teachers: Where a professor or teacher who is a resident of one of the contracting states visits the other contracting state for a period not exceeding two years for the purpose of teaching or carrying out advanced study or research at a university, college, school or other educational institution, any remuneration that person receives for such teaching, advanced study or research shall be exempt from tax in that other state to the extent to which such remuneration is subject to tax in the first-mentioned State.

P. Students and Trainees: Where a student or trainee, who is a resident of one of the contracting states or who was a resident of that state immediately before visiting the other contracting state and who is temporarily present in that other state solely for the purpose of his education or training, receives payments from sources outside that other state for the purpose of the his maintenance, education or training, those payments shall be exempt from tax in that other state.

7.6.4 Provisions Regarding Elimination of Double Taxation: In order to avoid double taxation it is provided that if a resident of India becomes liable to pay tax either directly or by deduction in the other country in respect of income from any source, he shall be allowed credit against the Indian tax payable in respect of such income to an amount not exceeding the tax borne by him in the other country on that portion of the income which is taxed in the said other country. The same benefit is available to the resident of the other country, on income taxed in India.

In respect of incomes on which taxes are either exempted or reduced, the country of residence will not take the exempted income into account while determining the tax to be imposed on the rest of the income.

7.6.5 Non-discrimination Clause: Most of the bilateral tax treaties have a non-discrimination clause which provides that the nationals of a contracting state shall not be subjected in the other contracting state to any taxation or any requirement connected therewith which is more burdensome than the taxation and connected requirements to which nationals of that other state in the same circumstances and under the same conditions are or may be subjected. The same holds for taxation on permanent establishment which an enterprise of a contracting state has in the other contracting state.

7.6.6 Mutual Agreement Procedure: Tax treaties lay down a mutual agreement procedure (MAP) for resolving disputes arising out of their application. The taxpayer may approach the competent authority of the contracting state of which he is a resident where he feels that the assessment to be made or order passed is not in accordance with the terms of the treaty. The competent authority shall endeavour to resolve the dispute by mutual agreement with the competent authority of the other contracting state, with a view to the avoidance of taxation which is not in accordance with the Agreement. (The case is normally required to be presented within two years from the first notification of the action which gives rise to taxation not in accordance with the Agreement).

The Central Board of Direct Taxes vide instruction of November 2002, has laid down the following procedure for giving effect to the resolution of dispute under MAP:

- Applicant shall be required to give an acceptance to the decision arrived at under MAP and that he will forego any right to appeal on the same issue.
- Where the issue is under appeal, the assessing officer shall also obtain an undertaking from the assessee regarding withdrawal of appeal on the issue.

7.6.7 Exchange of Information: Bilateral tax treaties provide that competent authorities of contracting states shall exchange such information as is necessary for applying the provisions of the treaty or of domestic laws of the contracting states concerning taxes covered by the treaty. This clause is included with a view to prevent fraud or evasion of taxes. It is further provided that any information received by a contracting state shall be treated as secret and shall be disclosed only to persons or authorities (including courts and administrative bodies) involved in the assessment or collection of, the enforcement or prosecution in respect of, or the determination of appeals in relation to the taxes which are the subject of the Convention. Such persons or authorities shall use the information only for such purposes but may disclose the information in public court proceedings or in judicial decisions.

The competent authorities shall, through consultation, develop appropriate conditions, methods and techniques concerning the matters in respect of which such exchanges of information shall be made, including, where appropriate, exchanges of information regarding tax avoidance.

7.7 Double Taxation Relief Where no Tax Treaty Exists

Section 91 grants unilateral relief from double taxation to

the residents in respect of foreign tax paid abroad. It is noteworthy that Section 91 comes into force only when relief is not available under Section 90. Following are the requirements of Section 91: (a) the assessee should be a resident of India in the previous year, (b) such income should not be deemed to accrue in India under the provisions of the Act, (c) the income should be taxed in both the countries and there is no double tax treaty with that country, and (d) the assessee should have in fact paid the tax in such foreign country either by deduction or otherwise.

Thus, if an Indian resident proves that tax has been paid in respect of his income which accrued or arose to him in the countries with which India has no agreement for double taxation relief, he is entitled to a deduction from the Indian income tax payable by him.

7.8 Issues Relating to Indo-Mauritius Tax Treaty

As tax treaties (or DTAAs) are country-specific, the contours of taxation and concessions granted vary based on the comparative advantage that India enjoys with them. In this context, Indo-Mauritius tax treaty has been of considerable concern. The trends indicate Mauritius as the top investing country in India. The fact that a small economy like Mauritius is the largest foreign investor in a huge economy like India surpassing developed nations like USA, Japan and UK calls for further investigation.

A study of the articles dealing with residency and taxation of capital gains reveals that special consideration was given to business entities of Mauritius (perhaps in view of the fact that Mauritius was a less developed country than India). The tax treaty with Mauritius was signed in August 1982. The treaty specified that capital gains made on the sale of shares of Indian companies by investors resident in Mauritius would be taxed only in Mauritius and not in India. For almost 10 years, the treaty existed only on paper since foreign institutional investors (FIIs) were not allowed to invest in Indian stock markets. This changed in 1992 when FIIs were allowed into India.

Coinciding with this liberalization of the Indian economy, the Government of Mauritius promulgated the Mauritius Offshore Business Activities Act, 1992 to regulate the offshore business in that country. This Act allowed foreign companies to register in Mauritius for investing abroad. A body corporate registered under the laws in Mauritius would be a resident in Mauritius and thus 'subject to taxation' as a resident. Income Tax Act of Mauritius provided that offshore companies were liable to pay 'zero percent' tax. Thus, by bringing an offshore company within the definition of resident, not only was the benefit of offshore company extended to it but also the benefits of residency allowable under the DTAA bestowed on it. This led to establishment of conduit companies in Mauritius through which investors of third countries routed their investment to India. By doing so, they avoided paying capital gains tax altogether and also enjoyed low rates of dividend and income taxes in Mauritius (Mauritius does not have a capital gains tax).

The above position has led to concern among tax authorities in India about the loss of rightful revenue. A Report of the Central Board of Direct Taxes observed, "In effect, the whole exercise of avoidance of double taxation turned out to be avoidance of taxation altogether." Two questions have been challenging the basis of the Indo-Mauritius tax treaty.

- Is India giving away much more in tax exemptions than it is getting in investments?
- Will investments come to India even if the lucrative routes through Mauritius don't exist?

The Joint Parliamentary Committee (that presented its 'Report on Stock Market Scam' to the Parliament on December 21, 2003) in its observation on the Indo-Mauritius tax treaty noted that "there could be substantial revenue loss due to the 'residency clause' in the Indo-Mauritius DTAA". It, therefore, recommended that companies investing in India through Mauritius should be required to file a declaration of ownership with RBI, to the effect that all the directors and effective management was in Mauritius.

7.8.1 Supreme Court on Indo-Mauritius DTAA: The tax authorities in India, recognizing the need to curtail the 'abuse' of the Indo-Mauritius treaty denied the benefit of the treaty (March 2000) to some offshore business companies (OBC) registered in Mauritius that had claimed exemption from tax under the Income Tax Act, by rejecting the certificate of residence furnished by them. Such OBCs were claiming exemption of capital gains from stock market operations, which gave the right of taxation of such capital gains to Mauritius.

At around the same time, there were fluctuations in the stock markets and general perception that the action of the department denying the benefit of Mauritius residency to some Mauritius based FIIs was the root cause for such fluctuations. It was projected that this would have or had resulted in huge outflows of foreign investment from India. To clear the doubts, as also clarify the intent of the Indo-Mauritius DTAA, the Central Board of Direct Taxes issued Circular 789 dated 13 April 2000 requiring, inter alia, the assessing officer to accept the certificate of residence granted under the local legislation of Mauritius to OBCs operating from third countries including India.

Considering a 'public interest litigation' (PIL), Delhi High Court quashed the above circular as bad in law on the grounds that the income tax officer was entitled to lift the corporate veil in order to ascertain whether a company was actually resident of Mauritius or not in exercise of his quasi-judicial powers and any attempt by the Board to interfere with this would be contrary to the intendment of the Act. In the aftermath of the Delhi High Court judgment foreign direct investment as well as portfolio flows nosedived. Very likely fund managers chose other investment destinations that continued to offer attractive tax concessions. What was needed in India was to plug the loopholes and not invalidate the beneficial provisions of the tax treaty.

The Supreme Court then upheld the sanctity of rules framed under bilateral tax treaties. The honourable Supreme Court in its judgment in the case of *Azadi Bachao Andolan* on 7th October 2003 upholding the issue of circular by the Board as also the Indo-Mauritius DTAA, held that:

- Indo-Mauritius DTAC (1983) is not 'ultra vires' of the powers of the Central Government under Section 90, on account of its susceptibility to "treaty shopping".
- Circular 789 of April 2000 issued by the Board falls within the parameters of the powers exercisable by the Board under Section 119. The circular does not in any way crib, cabin or confine the powers of the assessing officer with regard to any assessment. It merely formulates guidelines to be applied in the matters of assessment of assessees covered by the provisions of Indo-Mauritius DTAA.
- Merely because, at a given time there may be an exemption from income tax in respect of particular head of income, it is not correct to say that the taxable entity is not liable to taxation.

The Supreme Court took note of the fact that, "In recent years, India has been the beneficiary of significant foreign funds through the Mauritius Conduit. Although economic reforms in India since 1991 permitted such capital transfers, the amount would have been much lower without the India-Mauritius tax treaty". The Supreme Court's action in upholding the validity of the Circular had a number of positive implications for currency inflows into the country. Through the circular, the Central Board of Direct Taxes (CBDT) allowed investors incorporated in Mauritius to claim tax exemptions on their investments routed through that country.

During the pendency of the proceedings before the Supreme Court, the Board issued a circular on 10th February 2003 clarifying that where an assessing officer finds and is satisfied that an entity is resident of both India and Mauritius, he would be free to proceed to determine the residential status under the DTAA by invoking what is otherwise also known as the 'tie-breaker' clause. It further stated that where it was found that the company had its place of effective management in India, then, notwithstanding it being incorporated in Mauritius, *it would be taxed under the DTAA in India.*

In the context of the tax treaty, Finance Minister P. Chidambaram stated, "The government has no intention of introducing long-term capital gains tax or to carry out a one-sided review of the India-Mauritius tax avoidance treaty. The India-Mauritius treaty has been debated threadbare. Due to a host of economic, political and diplomatic reasons, we are not proposing any unilateral revision of the treaty".

The provisions of the Indo-Mauritius tax treaty continue to be a subject of debate. Despite the Supreme Court judgement quoted above and the assurance from the Finance Minister, there is still a section of legislators and bureaucrats who feel that India is giving away much more in tax exemptions than it is receiving in investments and that these tax concessions are uncalled for. In view of the above, it becomes imperative for the Government to constantly review the trends in foreign institutional investments and take adequate precautions to avoid investments by conduit companies formed with the primary purpose of taking advantage of the treaty.

7.9 Transfer Pricing Regulations in India

Taxing provisions for transfer pricing have become imperative, in the context of increasing participation of multinational groups in economic activities in India. However, transfer pricing solutions need to be flexible enough to adapt to the growing business of a multinational group, taking into account the organisation's perception of the risks of adverse tax assessments. Prior to April 2001, there were no detailed provisions in India relating to transfer pricing and determination of arm's length price. Foreign banks in India, for instance, are known to have shown profits after about one-third or even half of the actual profits were siphoned off under various global allocations, including head office costs. Even seemingly innocuous costs like research and development costs overseas, are often transfer pricing irregularities because of the price at which these transactions take place.

With globalisation of the Indian economy, a need was felt for a detailed and separate regulation for administering transfer pricing. Absence of such regulations not only results in litigation but loss of revenue to the exchequer as well. The Finance Minister, in his Budget speech (2000-01) stated, "The presence of multinational enterprises in India and their ability to allocate profits in different jurisdictions by controlling prices in intra-group transactions has made the issue of transfer pricing a matter of serious concern." In the same Budget, the Finance Minister announced that necessary legislative changes for transfer pricing will be made in the Finance Bill based on the recommendations of an Expert Group set up in November 1999.

The Finance Act, 2001 introduced detailed Transfer Pricing Regulations in India with effect from April 1, 2001 corresponding to the assessment year 2002-2003. The rules for transfer pricing were notified on August 21, 2001.

The sections and rules under the Income Tax Act dealing with transfer pricing regulations include Sections 92 to 92F, 271(1)(c), 271AA, 271BA , 271G and rules 10A to 10E.

7.10 Assessment and Collection of Tax from Non-residents in India

Notwithstanding the various concessions/exemptions given to non-residents under the income tax law, a stringent and pervasive system of assessment and collection of tax is followed. For example, the conditions laid down for the test of residence are not diluted and no relief is granted even if the stay of an assessee in India exceeds or falls short of the prescribed limits just by one day.

The income of a non-resident assessee is assessed for tax purposes either directly or indirectly (i.e. through his agent). The agent can either be a duly constituted agent or a person who can be treated as an agent. If therc is no duly constituted agent, the tax authorities are empowered to treat any of the following class of persons as the agent of a non-resident.

1. A person employed by or on behalf of the non-resident.
2. A person having a business connection with the non-resident.
3. A person from whom the non-resident is in receipt of any income either directly or indirectly.
4. A person who is trustee of the non-resident.
5. A person who has acquired any capital asset from a non-resident if that asset is situated in India.

It is noteworthy that any of the persons mentioned above and treated as agent should be in India at the time of assessment, though he need not necessarily be a resident in India. In other words, even a non-resident may be an agent for a non-resident assessee.

Still further, an agent may be a person who does not belong to any of the above-mentioned five categories. In short, any person may be treated as an agent of a non-resident if he has some connection with the income sought to be assessed. Under the law, there are elaborate guidelines concerning the appointment and liabilities of a duly constituted agent.

1. The agent is chargeable as a representative assessee of the non-resident for the incomes which are received or deemed to be received and accrue or are deemed to accrue in India.
2. The agent should have some connection with the income sought to be assessed in his hands even though the income belongs to the non-resident.
3. The agent is assessable for such incomes only as may belong to the non-residents and not to the residents.
4. The agent is assessed in the same manner and to the same extent as the non-resident himself would have been.
5. No one would be treated as an agent unless there is a liability to income tax on the non-resident.
6. The liability of the agent is personal and not conditional

upon his having in hand any funds of the profit of the non-resident.

A person who is treated as an agent of a non-resident is given an opportunity of being heard before he is treated as such. And if he is treated as the agent of a non-resident, he enjoys the right to deduct from the payments to the non-resident an amount equal to the tax estimated to be paid on the profits made by the non-resident in India.

The problem of tax recovery from the non-resident becomes more serious where there is no agent who can be made liable by the tax authorities for the purpose. To deal with such situations, the income tax law has devised the following two methods:

1. Deduction of tax at source.
2. Recovery of tax from assets.

Under the law, any income from salaries, interest on securities and dividends is subject to deduction of tax at source. The person responsible for paying such incomes is required to deduct income tax at source at the prescribed rates and deposit the same with the Government within the prescribed time limit. Deduction of tax at source is made on all such sums payable to a non-resident which are chargeable to income tax. Such sums may also include payments other than salaries, interest on securities and dividends [Section 195].

In case where there is no agent from whom the tax, payable by a non-resident, may be recovered or if it has not been deducted at source, the tax authorities are empowered to recover the tax from any assets of the non-resident which are in India or which may come to India any time later. Under the law there is no time limit for the recovery of a tax through this method.

The income tax law deals specifically with the assessment and collection of tax: (i) on profits of non-residents from shipping business, and (ii) on persons leaving India for good.

Cases may arise where non-residents are engaged in shipping business in India as the owners or charterers of ships without employing an agent from whom the tax on profits of such business can be recovered. To meet such cases the law provides that where a ship carries passengers or other items, 7.5 percent of the amount paid or payable in this respect to the owner or the charterer shall be deemed to be his income accruing in India for such carriage [Section 44B]. It is immaterial whether such an amount is paid or is payable in or out of India. Before leaving any port in India, the master of the ship has to prepare and furnish to the tax authorities a return of the full amount paid or payable to the owner or charterer of the ship in respect of the carriage of passengers or other items at that port since the last arrival of the ship there. This means the master of the ship is required to furnish a full account of carriage charges of the passengers etc. booked at the Indian port. On receipt of the return, the income tax officer has to assess the income and determine the amount of tax payable at the rates applicable to non-resident assessees.

The master of the ship may be exempted from furnishing such a return if the income tax officer is satisfied that the former has made satisfactory arrangement of furnishing the return and payment of tax through some other person acting on his behalf. As a cross-checking, port clearance is not granted to the ship until the collector of customs is satisfied that the tax assessable has been duly paid or that satisfactory arrangement for its payment has been made. Thus, cross-checking through inter-departmental co-operation is an important device to collect taxes from non-residents.

Another interesting provision of the income tax law pertains to the assessment and collection of tax from a person, resident or non-resident, who in the opinion of tax authorities, may leave India during the current assessment year for good [Section 230]. In such a case, the total income of that individual for the period from the expiry of the previous year up to the probable date of his departure from India is chargeable to tax in the same assessment year. [3] Where the income of such an individual cannot be determined properly, the income tax officer is authorised to estimate the same as per his own judgement without prejudice to the assessee. Individuals falling under this provision of the income tax law are required to obtain a tax clearance certificate from the foreign section of income tax office before leaving India.

End Notes

1. It relates to concurrent taxation powers enjoyed by different tiers of government in a federal polity. Concurrent taxation powers are a characteristic feature of fiscal federalism in USA, Canada, and Australia. Most tax fields in these countries are jointly occupied by the federal and provincial governments. Thus, personal income tax, corporation tax, general sales tax, and consumption tax (excise duty) are levied by the Federal as well as Provincial Governments in Canada. The only notable exception is the customs duties which belong exclusively to the Federal Government.

   The overlapping taxation powers often cause friction not only between the federal and provincial governments but also among the provinces *inter se* as regards the sharing of a tax base. The problem is solved through tax rental and tax sharing negotiations and agreements.

   In India, the Central and the State Governments have no concurrent powers of taxation. Taxes with inter-state base and those in the case of which all-India uniformity in rates is needed to facilitate industry and trade are vested in the Central Government. Taxes which are location-specific and relate to subjects of local consumption are with the States. The absence of joint occupancy of tax fields has successfully minimised double taxation, duplicate tax administration, and tax rivalry between the Centre and the States, and among the States themselves.
2. OECD, *Model Double Taxation Convention of Income and Capital*, 1977, p. 7.
3. Understandably, this is a departure from the general practice that the income of the previous year is to be assessed in the assessment year immediately following.

8

Summing Up

Prevention and control of black money generation is a pre-requisite to establish an equitable, transparent and a more efficient economy. Black money and tax evasion are eating into the social and moral fabric of Indian society. These two fiscal maladies are undermining the socio-economic objectives of India's Five Year Plans and are responsible for conspicuous and wasteful consumption, reduced savings, and increasing gap between the rich and the poor.

In recent years, the issue of corruption and black money has come in the forefront after a series of financial scandals. Generation of black money and its stashing abroad in tax havens and offshore financial centres have dominated discussions and debate in public fora during the recent past. Members of Parliament, the Supreme Court of India and the public at large have unequivocally expressed concern on the issue, particularly after some reports suggested estimates of such unaccounted wealth being held abroad.

After uproar in Parliament, Government of India came out with a *White Paper on Black Money* in May 2012. The *White Paper* presented the different facets of black money and its complex relationship with policy and administrative regime in the country. It also reflected upon the policy options and strategies that the Government had been pursuing to address the issue of black money and corruption in public life.

With liberalisation of restrictions on cross-border flow of goods and services and relaxation of foreign exchange control, new opportunities have opened up for tax evasion through tax havens, misuse of transfer pricing, and other sophisticated methods. Globalisation has reduced the cost of these sophisticated methods thereby facilitating generation of black money and its transfer across the border. These changes require new strategies to curb black money. The fight against generation and accumulation of black money is far more complex and prolonged, requiring stronger intervention of the state. It needs a robust legal framework, commensurate administrative set up, and a very strong resolve to fight the menace.

Following can be considered as essential requirements of a successful policy to unearth black money and curb tax evasion:

1. Given the democratic nature of governance in India, any long-term strategy to deal with black money and tax evasion must ensure public acceptance, broad-based political consensus and the commitment to implement it. In a federal structure of governance, this will require co-operation between agencies of the Central and State Governments.
2. In an increasingly globalized environment, it would need strong initiatives on the part of the Government to develop and strengthen mutual co-operation with the rest of the world. It would require institutionalisation and expansion of information exchange network at the international level to curb cross-border flow of illicit wealth. India should join the global crusade against black money.
3. Creation of effective administrative systems—using technology-based data processing—is necessary to generate actionable intelligence. Storage and exchange of information is an essential element of any scheme to control tax evasion. This is particularly so in a fast-growing economy like India where economic transactions are expanding fast. Storage and cross-checking of economic information through computer and related facilities is essential.
4. Creation of an appropriate legislative framework, and speedier judicial processes are needed to deal with illicit money and tax frauds.
5. Social sector schemes involving huge public expenditure under various programmes reportedly suffer from possible manipulations and leakages. Direct transfers [1] to the

accounts of beneficiaries can provide a solution, as it would prevent manipulations like bogus muster rolls etc.

Thus, a multi-pronged strategy is required to deal with the issue of generation of black money and its illicit transfer outside the country, and for bringing it back to India. The factors leading to generation of black money in India—along with the various measures attempted to counter it—make it clear that there is no single remedy to curb, control, and finally prevent the generation of black money. In fact, a comprehensive mix of well-defined strategies is needed by the Central and State Governments and put into practice by all their agencies in a co-ordinated manner.

8.1 Special Investigation Team (SIT) to Unearth Black Money, 2014

To meet the deadline set by the Honourable Supreme Court for the previous Government, the New Government of Prime Minister Narendra Modi constituted a Special Investigation Team (SIT), soon after assuming office on May 26, 2014. Headed by Justice M.B. Shah, a former judge of the Supreme Court, SIT was notified on May 27, 2014 to look into the issue of black money.

SIT, as ordered by the Court, will include the revenue secretary, directors of the Central Bureau of Investigation (CBI), Intelligence Bureau (IB), Research and Analysis Wing (RAW), Enforcement Directorate (ED), Chairman of the Central Board of Direct Taxes (CBDT), and a Deputy Governor of the Reserve Bank of India (RBI).

SIT has been charged with the responsibility and duties of investigation, initiation of proceedings and prosecution in some high-profile tax evasion cases.

The panel will have jurisdiction in cases where investigations have commenced, are pending or awaiting to be initiated or have been completed.

Terms of reference for the SIT require it to investigate "with respect to unaccounted monies being stashed in foreign banks by Indians or other entities operating in India that may arise in the course of such investigations and proceedings".

SIT will prepare a comprehensive action plan, including creation of an institutional structure that could enable the country to fight the battle against unaccounted money.

It may be recalled that on May 1, 2014 the Central Government had reported to the Supreme Court that investigations had been concluded against 18 of the 26 individuals that had bank accounts in Liechtenstein. It also said that these names were received from Germany and investigation had concluded in 17 cases of which no evidence was found against 8 and the investigation were concluded against them.

End Note

1. Government introduced Direct Benefit Transfer (DBT) plan on January 1, 2013. To begin with, benefits under 26 schemes will directly be transferred into the bank accounts of beneficiaries in 43 identified districts across respective states and union territories (UTs). Thus, benefits such as scholarships, pensions, and MGNREGA (Mahatma Gandhi National Rural Employment Guarantee Act) wages will be directly credited to the bank or post office accounts of identified beneficiaries. The DBT scheme will not substitute entirely for delivery of public services for now. It will replace neither food and kerosene subsidies under the TPDS (Targeted Public Distribution System) nor fertilizer subsidies. The DBT is designed to improve targeting, reduce corruption, eliminate waste, control expenditure, and facilitate reforms. Transfers that are already taking place through paper and cash mode will now be done through electronic transfers. This has been enabled by rapid roll out of Aadhar (Unique Identity) now covering 200 million people and rapidly growing to cover 600 million (nearly half of the population), with the National Population Register covering the other half of the populace. The DBT in tandem with such unique identification will ensure that the benefits reach the target groups faster and minimize inclusion and exclusion errors as well as corruption that are associated with manual processes.

   Banks will ensure that all beneficiaries in these districts have a bank account. All public sector banks (PSBs) and regional rural banks (RRBs) have made provision so that the data collected by the Departments/Ministries/Implementing agency concerned can be used for seeding the bank account details in the core banking system (CBS) of banks with Aadhaar. All PSBs have also joined the Aadhaar Payment Bridge of the National Payment Corporation of India for smooth transfer of benefits.

Appendices

Appendix 1

White Paper on Black Money

Government of India,
Ministry of Finance, May 2012

Strategies for Curbing Generation of Black Money

Note: *Generation of black money and its stashing abroad in tax havens and offshore financial centres have dominated discussions and debate in public fora during the recent past. Members of Parliament, the Supreme Court of India and the public at large have unequivocally expressed concern on the issue, particularly after some reports suggested estimates of such unaccounted wealth being held abroad.*

After uproar in Parliament, Government of India came out with a White Paper on Black Money in May 2012. The White Paper presented the different facets of black money and its complex relationship with policy and administrative regime in the country. It also reflected upon the policy options and strategies that the Government had been pursuing in the context of recent initiatives, or need to take up in the near future, to address the issue of black money and corruption in public life. Extracts from the White Paper are presented below.

Strategies for Curbing Generation of Black Money from Legal and Legitimate Activities

It would be fair to say that most of those involved in generation of black money are not indulging in activities that are criminal in themselves. For a business owner creating black money by evading taxes, preventive strategies need to reduce the incentives for evading taxes and create credible and effective deterrence. In essence, the strategies in such cases treat the person generating black money as a rational economic agent who can be made to comply with the law by creating appropriate incentives and disincentives in favour of reporting and tax compliance. Such a strategic mix will consist of the following four different pillars.

A. Reducing disincentives against voluntary compliance.
B. Reforms in vulnerable sectors of the economy.
C. Creating effective credible deterrence.
D. Supportive measures.

A. Reducing Disincentives against Voluntary Compliance

There can be several factors that disincentivise a person against reporting her/his income or wealth. Primarily, they consist of the cost that the person incurs in complying with the law and its reporting regulations. These costs consist of two major components, the tax that needs to be paid as part of the compliance and the costs that need to be incurred in addition to the taxes for complying with the regulatory obligations. Both of them are important disincentives and reducing them can improve disclosure and lessen the generation of black money.

A.1 Rationalization of Tax Rates: One of the most important factors in ensuring tax compliance is the tax rate. The Laffer curve [1] postulates that when the tax rates on producer surplus approach 100 percent, then tax revenues may approach zero, since economic agents would not be left with any incentive to produce. The higher the tax rate, higher is the disincentive against tax compliance and greater the propensity to generate black money. Thus, reducing tax rates, particularly the maximum marginal rates of progressive taxes, can increase tax revenue in two ways, first by increasing tax base and second by increasing compliance with the tax rules and thus can be one of the major policy tools for curbing the generation of black money.

In the past two decades, India has followed the approach of gradually bringing down tax rates of all major taxes imposed by the central government. The rising tax revenues as a result of this approach reflect the greater voluntary compliance and apparent success of the policy measures.

While rationalization of tax rates remains one of the fundamental and core strategies for curbing black money generation, the long-term success of this simple approach is dependent upon other strategic pillars that include creation of credible deterrence and necessary changes in public perception about tax evasion. If the tax administration is relatively weak, no tax rate changes can ensure compliance.

A.2 Reducing Transaction Costs of Compliance and Administration: The high transaction costs associated with compliance with the law and regulation is the other major disincentive that hinders compliance and pushes people towards generation of black money. It includes the opportunity cost of time and resources to the tax payer and tax administration. In a way these costs are far more significant than the tax, because unlike taxes, which are in the nature of transfer from the private to the public sector, these costs are real costs to the society.

The transaction costs consist of the costs of compliance, which are borne by the citizens or taxpayers and the costs of administration, which are incurred by the state, but eventually borne by the citizens by way of taxes that finance such expenditure. Among the two, the costs of compliance are generally more important since they are incurred by a larger number of economic agents. Interestingly, while the budgetary process and administrative and regulatory oversights are highly effective in controlling the costs of tax administration, the same may not always be the case with the costs of compliance.

Given the fact that the costs of compliance can be a major disincentive against compliance and reporting, reducing them will remain one of the most significant aspects of any strategy mix directed against black money generation. In the area of tax administration, the cost of collection in India has traditionally been one of the lowest in the world, remaining below 1 percent for several years now. In most developed economies, such costs hover around 1 to 2 percent.

The low cost of collection in Indian tax administration can be interpreted both as a positive achievement (due to lower burden on the exchequer) as well as negative development as it suggests lack of infrastructure and resources available to tax administrations, which in turn induces increased cost of compliance for the taxpayer. It may be possible in India too to significantly cut down the costs of compliance borne by the citizens, by raising the cost of administration to some extent. Simply put, investments in improving administrative facilitation of compliance with tax and other regulatory measures may lead to positive gains for the society.

One of the major opportunities for reduction in transaction costs has been created by the recent advancements in the area of information and communication technology. Both the direct and indirect tax administrations have significantly brought down the costs of compliance by various measures of e-governance, electronic reporting, e-filing of refunds, computerized central processing of returns, and electronic issue and transfer of refunds. This has become possible due to the successful allocation of PAN numbers and use of electronic services. Future strategies should strive for further development of electronic and net-based services and for improving the resources of tax administration, with the ultimate aim of reducing the cost of compliance for the taxpayer.

A.3 Further Economic Liberalization: Non-tariff barriers to economic activity are generally worse than tariff barriers. Where one cannot get a permit to undertake a legitimate activity, the transaction costs approach infinity, and create insurmountable incentives for unreported and unaccounted activities that will inevitably generate black money. The successive waves of economic liberalization during the last two decades have attempted to do away with such non-tariff barriers. The process must be relentlessly continued. The Electronic Delivery of Services Bill, 2011 that seeks to provide for electronic delivery of public services by the government to all persons to ensure transparency, efficiency, accountability, accessibility, and reliability in delivery of such services has been tabled before Parliament in December 2011. Once it is enacted, it will provide a major impetus towards this objective. Together, these measures can significantly cut down the transaction costs of compliance with the regulatory regime and reduce the disincentives against voluntary compliance, thereby restricting the generation of black money from legitimate economic activities.

B. Reforms in Vulnerable Sectors of the Economy

It can be seen from the discussions in the earlier sections that a large proportion of black money is generated from certain vulnerable sectors of economy, suggesting that effective reforms in those sectors can be a major strategy for curbing generation of black money in future. One of the best examples in this regard is gold trading, which was one of the major sources of black money generation and even crime prior to the reforms induced in that sector. While gold inflows into India remain persistently high, gold smuggling is no longer the menace as it used to be a few decades earlier. Similar or more effective reforms of other vulnerable sectors like real estate can yield a significant dividend in the form of reducing generation of black money in the long-term.

B.1 Financial Sector: The financial sector is the most important sector in the economy when it comes to transfer of funds generated through whatever means into further productive activities. Therefore, it is one sector that cannot possibly remain untouched by black money. Often black money enters it as part of financial instruments or other processes, which at times involve money laundering thereby highlighting the potential of this sector in detection and prevention of black money along with its sources and perpetrators. Fine tuning of financial regulation therefore remains one of the key areas in creating deterrence against generation of black money and detecting black money in the process of being laundered.

Significant progress made in the efficacy of the oversight

mechanism for financial markets needs to be pursued further. For this purpose, it is essential that the relevant authorities are able to get trained manpower with proper domain knowledge of financial investigation and oversight. One of the solutions could be to place efficient officials with requisite domain knowledge and skills from the financial investigative agencies in the operations/vigilance machinery of banks and financial institutions to keep proper vigil and ensure that rules and regulations are followed in these institutions.

In the last two decades, many foreign entities, including banks, financial institutions, and fund transfer entities have established businesses in India. A Committee headed by the Chairman, CBDT, has recently reported that Indian tax residents have been carrying out substantial monetary transactions through these entities or with their branches abroad. The Committee also recommended that India insist on entities operating in the country to report all global transactions above a threshold limit. For this purpose, appropriate laws, rules or contractual/licensing arrangements with these entities may be framed and implemented, as has been done in some other countries. In the Finance Bill, 2012, a beginning has been made by making filing of return of income mandatory for every resident (excluding not ordinary residents) having any assets or banking accounts located outside India even if s/he does not have a taxable income. Return forms have been notified in this regard. Similar strengthening of other reporting regimes can allow appropriate systems for flagging of dubious transactions in future and improve the probability of their timely detection and prevention.

B.2 Real Estate: The real estate sector in India constitutes about 11 percent of the GDP. Investment in property is a common means of parking unaccounted money and a large number of transactions in real estate are not reported or are under-reported. This is mainly on account of very high levels of property transaction taxes, commonly in the form of stamp duty. High transaction taxes in property are one of the biggest impediments to the development of an efficient property market. With tax rates of over 5 percent being imposed as stamp duty on buying of property, which otherwise also involves high transactions costs in terms of search, advertising, commissions, registration, and contingent costs related to title disputes and litigation, the property market remains one of the most inefficient asset markets in India. Unless the underlying distortions in this market are taken care of by appropriate reforms, it may be difficult to prevent such misuse.

As per the division of powers between the states and the centre, the real estate sector has largely been left to the state governments to regulate and tax. Even after the 73rd and 74th amendments to the constitution of India which recognized local rural and urban bodies as the third tier of government, the power to legislate with respect to real estate properties and transactions therein remains with the states. Different state governments have undertaken reforms in this sector at differing pace, while their implementation is further subject to the capacity and commitment of the respective local urban bodies.

The role of the central government in reforms of the real estate sector is generally limited and advisory in nature. However, this has not prevented the Government of India from initiating steps to incentivize reforms. Its flagship programme, the Jawaharlal Nehru National Urban Renewal Mission (JNNURM), being implemented since 2005-06 aims to support urban infrastructural development by providing both monetary and non-monetary support, for reforms in different sectors of the local economy. It includes reforms of the stamp duty regime to restrict it to no more than 5 percent. Some states have carried out this reform, but others are still persisting with very high stamp duty regimes. For states that are resource constrained there is a case for identifying and implementing adequate revenue-neutral substitutes to facilitate the rationalisation of stamp duties.

There are many other pending reforms required for the emergence of an efficient competitive real estate market. These include repeal of the Urban Land Ceiling Regulation Act (ULCRA), reforms of the Rent Control Act that will balance the interests of tenants and owners and free properties of its distortions, revision of bye-laws to streamline the approval process for construction of buildings, development of sites, simplification of legal and procedural frameworks for conversion of land from agricultural to non-agricultural purposes, introduction of the property title certification system in urban local bodies, introduction of computerised process of registration of land and property, introduction of e-governance in local administration and tax payments, creation of computerised fiscal cadastres and rationalisation of property tax designs.

Each of these areas had been given a thrust by making it conditional to the release of financing for urban projects by the central government. Evidence suggests that the mission has achieved considerable success. However, a lot more needs to be done in this regard. There may also be a case for integration of local urban authorities in a nationwide digital database and sharing of data and information with state and central agencies.

The current provisions of the direct tax legislation provide for mandatory furnishing of the tax identification number by the buyer and seller of an immovable property if the value exceeds ₹ 5 lakh.

Also, every registry of property is required to furnish annually information regarding transactions in immovable property if the value exceeds ₹ 30 lakh. However, as many registrar offices still operate on a manual system, there are a number of gaps and lapses in the reporting of such transactions.

To reduce the element of black money in transactions relating to immovable property and facilitate focused action based on actionable intelligence by monitoring agencies, simple reporting systems can be evolved that will facilitate the development of a nationwide database. Such a database should be computer-driven with minimal interface between the authorities and the people, and accessible to all financial regulatory authorities.

One of the measures for deterring use of the real estate sector for generation and investment of black money could be the provision of deducting tax at source on payments made on real estate transactions and mandating it as a pre-condition for registering of the transacted property. The provisions of tax collected at source on the developers of the property can also be considered as a possible policy measure. Electronic payment and electronic reporting can mitigate the compliance burden.

Further, to reduce the element of black money in transactions relating to immovable property, the provision of no objection certificate (NOC) may be introduced in the income tax law with safeguards to reduce administrative complications and increased ease of compliance, so that an appropriate and uniform database is set up and a proper national-level regulation also put in place. The new system should be computer-driven with minimal interface between the tax authorities and taxpayers, and enforced by a dedicated unit within the investigative machinery of the income tax department on the basis of pre-determined parameters and standard operating procedures.

B.3 Bullion and Jewellery Sector: Bullion and jewellery is an important sector for both generation and consumption of black money and is also targeted by black money holders looking towards protecting the value of their black money from inflationary depreciation. Moreover, a fairly large number of transactions in this sector remain totally unreported and therefore facilitate investment and consumption of black money.

There is also urgent need to improve the reporting and monitoring systems in this sector. Since there are a number of financial laws already applicable to such businesses, it can be achieved to some extent through amendments to or modifications of the laws governing income tax, and customs duty. In this regard, the Income Tax Act has made it mandatory to obtain PAN or Form 60/Form 61 for purchase of bullion above ₹ 5 lakh. However, given the need to catch all transactions, the best bet would be the proposed GST Act. This is an area that needs careful analysis in terms of efficacy and assessment of costs and benefit before the required regulations are enacted.

B.4 Cash Economy: Cash has always been a facilitator of black money since transactions made in cash do not leave any audit trail. So far, efforts to regulate and control cash transactions have been constrained due to two reasons. The first is that the poor have to deal in cash, particularly in the rural sector, and accordingly payments on account of labour wages or those made to rural artisans and institutions need to be made in cash. Second, the costs of transaction imposed by any regulations are likely to spread across the economy and affect both consumers and producers, thereby leading to resistance and lack of support for such a move.

However, given the primary importance of cash in relation to both generation and use of black money, there is no alternative but to target cash transactions in a way that will not affect those complying with the law, while making it difficult for those intending to generate and utilise black money. This will require keeping fairly high transaction limits and exempting those with a reasonable audit trail at either end of the transactions. Further work needs to be done in this regard in future by way of legal curbs and regulations that can restrict the generation and flow of black money within the economy.

As of now there are no legal restrictions to keeping very large amounts of cash with oneself or transporting it from one place to another. One is neither required to report it nor provide any explanation for it. There have been suggestions that the government may consider amending existing laws, including the Coinage Act, 2011, The Reserve Bank of India Act, 1934, FEMA, and the Indian Penal Code, or enacting an entirely new statute aimed at regulating the possession and transportation of cash above a particular threshold limit. This may include creating a limitation on cash holdings for private use, as well as provisions for confiscation of cash held beyond such prescribed limits. However, such laws need a broader political consensus to emerge for their acceptance in Parliament.

Another important measure in this regard could be the promotion of banking channels including use of credit and debit cards, since they leave adequate audit trails and hence disincentivise black money generation. The opposite is true of trade practices that block the audit trail, such as cheque discounting, which can be discouraged applying the same logic. With electronic transfer facilities being available to trade, one can foresee this as one of the major thrusts towards strengthening accountability and discouraging unaccounted activities.

Towards this end, some important initiatives have already being taken which include the reduction of the validity period of cheques and demand drafts from six to three months with effect from 1st April 2012, which will discourage discounting of negotiable instruments. Payments by debit and credit cards through Indian e-service intermediaries like 'RuPay' [2] can further bring down the costs of using such cards, improve their acceptability, and thereby encourage payments in these modes and reduce the cash economy. It is imperative that payment of wages and salaries in the private sector should also be through banking channels and should become cashless, in line with the government objective of financial inclusion. Government can also deliberate providing tax incentives for use of credit/debit cards as practised in Republic of Korea. Provisions for collection of tax at source at a low level on cash purchases may also be considered as a possible policy option.

B.5 Mining and Allocation of Property Rights over Natural Resources: Natural Resources including mines, forests, land, water, and spectrums belong to the country as a whole, but their efficient allocation and utilization demands that government assigns property rights to private parties in lieu of financial payments made to the public exchequer. This process calls for significant improvement in transparency and public accountability and appropriate price discovery mechanisms, in the absence of which these sectors can become vulnerable to illegal encroachments, while their allocation at highly subsidised rates can lead to windfall gains for the allottees. There is therefore need for comprehensive reforms requiring coordination and consensus among states and the centre.

In order to ensure transparent and efficient allocation of natural and man-made resources, oversight in the form of comprehensive regulations, independent regulator, and appointment of ombudsmen for grievance redressal, particularly for scarce resources—as in land, minerals, and forests—can be considered as a remedy.

B.6 Equity Trading: While equity trading has witnessed large-scale reforms during the last couple of decades, it has also seen new challenges being faced by the regulators consisting of cartel-based price manipulation and profiteering, proxy investments through conduits, and routing of investments through tax havens in case of FIIs. Among these, the issue of investing through tax havens is dealt with subsequently, but there are many other areas in this sector that need further reforms.

The RBI has already strengthened the implementation of KYC norms. In this regard, there have been suggestions that it could consider stricter implementation of these norms and limit the number of accounts that can be introduced by a single person and the number of accounts that can be maintained in the same branch by any entity and maintain vigilance about the same address being used for opening accounts in different names. Stricter adherence to, and enforcement of, KYC norms can help ensure proper compliance by banks and financial institutions. The government, as well as the RBI, also needs to put a better regulatory framework in place and act promptly against errant persons/institutions.

To prevent misuse of 'off-market' and 'dabba-trading' or trading outside the recognised stock exchanges, further amendments in the income tax law may need to be introduced to allow losses in off-market share transactions to be set off only against profits derived from such transactions. Such a measure may create barriers to misuse of such trading and plug an important loophole for generation of black money.

B.7 Misuse of Corporate Structure for Generation of Black Money: The various ways in which corporate structure can be misused to evade taxes have already been discussed in detail in preceding chapters. It would suffice to state here that efforts made by the Government of India to create greater transparency and facilitate exchange of information need to be carried further. There is also need to create a robust database of remittances made by corporates out of India and carry out an analysis of their backward and forward linkages in order to understand the nature and legitimacy of the transmitted funds. The FIU-IND may be empowered by law to receive reports (similar to other reports submitted to it) on all international fund transfers through the Indian financial system, on the lines of the FIUs of Australia and Canada.

B.8 Non-Profit Organisations and the Cooperative Sector: There are several fiscal and regulatory privileges under different laws available to non-profit and cooperative organisations. Their income, subject to various conditions, is treated differently for taxation purposes from that of privately owned profit-oriented concerns. This creates incentives for potential evaders to camouflage their concerns as non-profitable, charitable, or cooperative in nature. This can only be dealt with through a multi-pronged strategy of reducing the privileges available to them on one hand and subjecting them to a stricter regulatory regime on the other. However, given the role of genuine NPOs in the welfare of the downtrodden and the broader government policy of supporting such endeavours, this is a somewhat complex issue that may easily evoke strong emotional responses and hence can be implemented only after a larger consensus is reached within society.

At present, no government agency has a complete database of NPOs. The CBDT has the largest such database. There may be information with other agencies such as the Ministry of Home Affairs and the CEIB. It has been suggested that the CBDT may be assigned the role of a centralized agency with which every NPO would be required to be registered and by which it would be allotted a unique number. This would be in line with the decision taken by the government in light of the possible misuse of the sector for undesirable activities. Suggestions made by the NPO Sector Assessment Committee, an Inter-ministerial body, should be accepted and the office of the Director General of Income Tax (Exemption) appropriately strengthened in terms of manpower, infrastructure, and capacity building.

The regulation and enforcement of KYC norms in the cooperative sector may be strengthened by the state governments as well as the central government. Responsibility may be fixed for any lapse in this regard as well as for any subsequent failure to alert authorities as regards any suspicious transactions in such accounts.

C. Creating Effective Credible Deterrence

Since neither the tax rates nor the transaction costs of compliance can be brought down to zero, there will always remain a certain incentive for generation of black money, which can only be tackled by having effective credible deterrence in place. The reason why deterrence is placed third in this list of strategies is not because it is less important than the previous strategies but because it works in tandem with the strategies mentioned earlier. To exemplify, deterrence that is created with huge compliance costs can turn out to be counterproductive since the disincentive against generation of black money will be overshadowed by the disincentive against compliance resulting from high transaction costs.

Similarly, if the tax rates remain very high along with restrictions and barriers in economic activities, the level of deterrence that will be required to offset the consequently high incentives for evasion and non-compliance will be very difficult to achieve. Finally, very high levels of deterrence based on severe penalties or punishments create further distortions of incentives and can result in rent-seeking behaviour requiring additional levels of monitoring, supervision, surveillance, and litigation, all of which add to transaction costs and further increase the incentives for evasion and non-compliance.

It is this complex interplay of factors that the monitoring agencies responsible for creation of effective deterrence are required to address. With a rapidly growing and a globalising economy, and with developments in information technology and networking, the technological challenges are becoming ever more complex. All these challenges need to be tackled by multi-pronged strategies discussed in the following paragraphs.

C.1 Integration of Databases Leading to Actionable Intelligence by Monitoring Agencies: Modern administration and investigation must be focused on collecting all relevant data, its seamless and automated collection from different sources under different laws and regulations, and its integration into a collective national database. It should generate meaningful information that can be processed into actionable intelligence by the respective state agencies for their respective purposes. This will ensure that their actions are focused and well targeted, thereby ensuring that investigations are directed towards potential evaders while those complying with laws and regulations do not have to bear any additional costs of scrutiny or investigations. Though different state agencies are already coordinating their actions to tackle the menace of black money with considerable success, there is need for further integrating the systems and databases of different agencies to avoid the duplication of efforts and formulation of a coherent and effective strategy for combating black money.

Efforts are already being made to integrate the systems and organisations of different agencies. Taxpayers are required to file different kinds of returns and reports based on their tax liability such as returns of income and wealth tax, tax deducted at source (TDS), international remittances, and of international transactions with associated enterprises, tax audit reports, and reports of international transactions. The information obtained through all these returns and forms is compiled in the database of the Income Tax Department. Information is also collected from different agencies such as banking and financial institutions, registrars of immovable properties, land records office, mutual fund organisations, and credit card agencies as per the provisions of the Income Tax Act. All this information is stored in the database of the Income tax Department. Based on this information, the system selects cases for scrutiny every year. The future strategies should strive to further strengthen the ability to flag potential evaders by processing the database.

Similar systems and databases are being maintained by other government agencies as well. For example, banks maintain individual accounts and have information about each and every banking transaction of taxpayers. The Customs and Excise Department has the information related to exports, imports, and manufacturing. The information available with all these Departments and agencies is required to be integrated on real-time basis subject to confidentiality provisions of various Acts. This is a real challenge considering the huge taxpayer base of India and the huge data available with each and every department/agency. It requires a common taxpayer identifier and real-time connectivity of the systems of different agencies. The integration exercise further requires regular updating of the database and safeguards against the misuse of the data.

This coordination is required at all levels including the generation, layering, and introduction/accumulation of black money. The integration has to be through legal provisions, systems, organizations as well as at informal level. The Government of India has introduced different legal provisions for improving the coordinated efforts. The introduction of VAT and the proposal to introduce the GST are examples of such measures. It is common knowledge that one of the major sources of generation of black money is the out of books sales. These out of books sales are resorted to by taxpayers to evade different taxes such as excise duty, sales tax, and income tax. With the introduction of VAT, the credit of the duty on the input can be claimed only if VAT has been paid thereon. Thus it discourages out of books sales. In the earlier system, e-tax was required to be paid at the point of first sale in the state and thereafter the goods became tax paid. Thus, no sales tax was required to be paid on the resale of goods. Now each vendor has to pay taxes on the addition by him to the value of the goods. This ensures better reporting and discourages the generation of black money. The introduction of the GST will be a major step in the integration of the efforts of different agencies dealing with black money.

The information and intelligence gathering mechanisms of various economic agencies need to be more broad-based so that the entire gamut of economic activity is captured in an electronic manner, mined, and analysed. All the agencies continuously need to get technologically upgraded in this area to effectively tackle the menace of black money. The skills of manpower resources available with the agencies also need to be upgraded continuously and exposed to global best practices in their sphere of work.

C.2 Strategies to Strengthen Direct Tax Administration: As the contribution of direct taxes in revenue collections rises, direct tax administration must be strengthened to ensure that it keeps pace with the rising needs of the growing economy. This factor is also important because direct tax databases are one of the largest databases available in the country and being an accounts-based tax, it has the potential of creating appropriate audit trails that can build strong deterrence against evasion as well as help catch evaders and trace black money kept in various forms both within the country and abroad. There are several measures that are likely to form an inherent part of this strategy and they are discussed in the following paragraphs.

Direct tax administration has a major role to play in the process of unearthing black money. The personnel manning the department need to be properly equipped for discharging this role. Scrutiny assessment of the returns of income is an important tool for detecting money on which payment of any taxes is being evaded. However, it needs to be complemented by the ability of the tax administration to prosecute the evaders by collecting appropriate evidence against them. In order to achieve this objective, a lot of capacity building will need to be undertaken as the requirements of criminal investigation are quite different from those of civil scrutiny. The Directorate of Criminal Investigation, if provided the right training, infrastructure, powers, and resources, may become a very effective deterrent against tax evasion and black money.

The large taxpayer units (LTU) handles cases of corporates having presence at several locations. This office plays a crucial role in the tax scrutiny of large taxpayers. One crucial aspect of the functioning of the LTU is coordinated functioning of the income tax and the excise departments. This enables in-depth analysis of the finances of big corporates and helps prevent tax evasion. The LTU may become more effective if the audit cycle of the income tax, service tax and excise departments is aligned. Presently, these three agencies are under the umbrella of the LTU. However, they scrutinise different accounting periods at the same time. This reduces the scope of the simultaneous scrutiny and examination of the assessee. Further, there is a need for special training of the officers and staff members to make them aware of issues relating to big corporate houses. The officers need to be trained in the enterprise resource planning (ERP) software implemented by these large taxpayers. The books of accounts of the big corporate houses are generally maintained under this software which requires special skills for verification and unearthing of tax evasion. With the introduction of the GST, VAT may also come under the umbrella of the LTU making it all the more effective.

The Directorate of International Taxation has played a crucial role in unearthing black money by detecting mis-pricing in international transactions with associated enterprises. The Directorate has unearthed a number of such transactions in the recent past and has brought them to tax. However, the manpower and the technology available to the Directorate need to be improved.

Under the provisions of the Income Tax Act, 1961, there is a requirement for specified entities to report high value transactions through AIRs. The department has received significant information involving suspected unreported income through AIRs. In a large proportion of these cases, the transactions do not contain valid PANs. Analysis reveals that in many cases, companies have not filed income tax returns even though they are live and TDS has been deducted in such cases. Similar analysis reveals that though data is available in the Department that can throw up cases where returns are not being filed though such entities are deriving income during the relevant year, appropriate action is sometimes constrained for want of adequate manpower.

Given the importance of TDS in modern tax administration, there is urgent need to both plug the manpower gaps as well as strengthen systems for TDS monitoring and its integration in terms of data with existing databases. On the lines of the central processing centres (CPCs) which are already functional and gradually dealing with the bulk of processing of returns of income, CPCs are envisaged for TDS too, which will make TDS monitoring far more efficient, thereby also collecting more data and creating greater audit trail of transactions in the economy, which itself is a major deterrent against tax evasion and non-compliance of reporting regulations.

Till date, PAN has been allotted to more than 11 crore entities while income tax returns have been filed by 3.5 crore entities. There is thus a huge gap between the number of entities to whom PAN has been allotted vis-à-vis the number of deductors filing income tax returns. The Parliamentary Standing Committee for Finance has pointed to this gap and advised the Department to take suitable action. Such action again needs adequate manpower as well as persistent action towards ensuring that the provisions of PAN are implemented and accurately complied with.

Similarly, around 3 crore pieces of CIB information are uploaded into the system which contains financial data of taxpayers. The data includes substantial percentage of cases where PAN has not been reported by the taxpayer entities. This data needs to be efficiently processed using computerised systems to create meaningful information and actionable intelligence. These involve further sophistication of underlying systems as well as follow up action, both of which require further manpower with adequate expertise. Providing adequately trained manpower can help improve the efficiency of the Department by leaps and bounds.

The data-mining capacities of the Department need to be strengthened with risk-analysis tools. Due to the voluminous data coming for analysis from different sources, the work cannot be done manually and intelligent software needs to be designed to this end. There is also need for setting up a Directorate of Risk Management.

C.3 Strengthening of the Prosecution Mechanism: Sometimes taxpayers may be willing to take a calculated risk of tax evasion and may even justify it as a 'commercial risk'. Such calculated risk taking may be more effectively deterred by effective prosecution.

The Income Tax Act, 1961, has elaborate procedure for criminal prosecution. For instance, if a taxpayer wilfully attempts to evade payment of any tax, interest, or penalty, he may be subject to rigorous imprisonment of six months to seven years and fine, if the tax sought to be evaded is more than ₹ 1,00,000. Further, prosecution can be launched for various other offences such as making false statements or withholding tax. In case an offence is committed by a company, Indian or foreign, every person who at the time of commission of such offence was in charge of, or was responsible for the company in the conduct of its business is deemed to be guilty and is liable for prosecution. However, despite these provisions being in the statute, the actual state of criminal prosecution in tax matters in India is somewhat dismal. In very few cases, do the tax authorities opt for prosecution and subsequent conviction in tax evasion cases is rare and cannot be found even in high-profile search cases. The absence of a specialized prosecution wing and the cumbersome procedure contribute to this state of affairs.

The government has taken a number of corrective steps in the recent past. A Directorate of Criminal Investigation has been established to perform functions in relation to offences listed under the Income Tax Act and will act as a specialized arm of the government dealing with criminal prosecution in case of tax evasion. The Finance Bill, 2012, provides for constitution of special courts for trial of offences under the Income Tax Act. Judges having specialized knowledge in tax matters can be appointed to preside over the special courts for speedy disposal of cases.

Further, it reduces the maximum punishment prescribed under various offences from three years to two years for simplification of the trial. Offences carrying maximum punishment of more than two years are subject to 'warrant case' procedure which is more time consuming compared to offences carrying a punishment of less than two years which are subject to 'summons case' procedure which is much quicker and thus will result in quicker trial. The Finance Bill, 2012, also provides for appointment of specialized public prosecutors for representing the case of tax authorities before the courts.

C.4 Enhanced Exchange of Information: With increased globalisation and liberalisation of national economies and removal/relaxation of control of foreign investments/foreign exchange, there has been manifold increase in cross-border transactions giving taxpayers greater opportunities for tax evasion and avoidance compared to taxpayers operating only in domestic markets. While the taxpayers operate globally, the tax administrators remain confined to their respective jurisdictions. Thus, to effectively tackle the tax evasion/avoidance adopted by taxpayers, it is imperative that tax administrators cooperate with each other. A key element of such international cooperation in tax matters is through the exchange of information mechanism entered into by countries by way of DTAAs and TIEAs as also through multilateral instruments for exchanging information.

The officers of the income tax department can use the legislative framework to obtain information from foreign jurisdictions by seeking details such as ownership across the layers of corporate chains, formation documents and subsequent updates, details of beneficiaries and other terms in cases of trusts, accounting records and statements, banking information, and tax returns.

Simultaneously, there is need for capacity building among our tax officers for expediently utilizing information exchange networks. A manual on exchange of information addressing these issues is under preparation. Further, as the exchanges with foreign jurisdictions will increase substantially, a computerized EOI cell is therefore being created in the FT&TR Division of CBDT, with two director-level and four under secretary-level officers. This EOI cell, designed on the lines of best practices followed by other countries, is developing a comprehensive database of inbound and outbound exchanges, a high level of security, and the facility of electronic exchange with competent authorities of other countries. The EOI cell needs to be fully integrated with the Income Tax Department and other investigation agencies. It can also be utilized to obtain administrative assistance in different matters such as exchange of information, assistance in tax collection, tax examination abroad, simultaneous tax examination, and service of documents. The EOI cell is also planning to integrate itself with the systems of other countries. This will help reduce the time lag in the exchange of information.

C.5 Income Tax Overseas Units: To facilitate international cooperation in areas of exchange of information, transfer pricing, and taxation of cross-border transactions, ITOUs have been opened with the objectives of monitoring issues related to double taxation avoidance, assistance in handling issues arising out of international taxation and transfer pricing, expediting negotiation of TIEAs with tax havens and non-cooperative jurisdictions, facilitating expedient exchange of information, and facilitating mutual assistance in collection of taxes. These units need to be expediently and optimally utilised for matters related to taxes as well as exchange of information in order to curb black money.

The way forward for the ITOUs is coordination with the competent authority office of the foreign country on real-time basis on mutual administrative assistance in tax matters including the exchange of information, assistance in tax collection, simultaneous tax examination, tax examination abroad, and service of documents. The ITOUs will also assist the competent authority with resolving cases under mutual agreement procedures and advanced pricing agreements.

C.6 Efforts to be Undertaken at International Forums: India needs to continue raising issues for enhanced transparency and co-operation amongst jurisdictions. Some of these issues include automatic exchange of information, sharing of past information, country-wise reporting, registers of beneficial ownership, and need for toolbox of counter measures.

C.7 International Taxation and Transfer Pricing: International taxation and transfer pricing are new focus areas both to check the menace of black money and for augmentation of tax collection. By shedding some light upon the dark side of international taxation and transfer pricing in the previous chapter, we have stimulated a closer and more critical consideration of the ramifications of transfer pricing and international taxation practices and thereby highlighted the need to make their administration more effective. The Government has already introduced the Advance Pricing Agreement (APA) in the financial year 2012-13. The APA is an instrument through which the arms' length price of an international transaction will be determined in advance. This will not only ensure avoidance of trade mis-pricing but will also ensure that there is tax certainty for the MNEs located in India or doing business with India. There is also need to step up research into multi-layered cross-border transactions and ever-changing transfer-pricing manipulations to prevent considerable opportunities for capital flight, tax avoidance, and generation and transfer of black money.

C.8 Effective Curbing of Structuring through Tax Havens: India has consistently taken the stand against structuring of transactions through tax havens by creating a complex chain of subsidiaries for avoidance of taxes. Indian tax administration has always been of the view that foreign investors in India should pay taxes on their income either in India or the country of their residence, and does not endorse attempts to avoid taxes in both the countries by use of such opaque tax-avoidance structures. The legislative measures included in the Finance Bill, 2012, and the introduction of GAAR can create necessary deterrence against such structuring and thereby plug this loophole for tax evasion.

C.9 Strengthening of Indirect Tax Administration: Indirect tax administration has undergone major reforms during the last two decades. Most of these pertain to rationalisation of custom duties on international trade and they have indirectly contributed to the economic growth in recent times. Another important development in the field of indirect taxation is the introduction of service tax, which is now contributing significantly to the central government's revenue collections. Liberalization of international trade and dilution of tariff barriers have significantly reduced the incentives for black money generation, but not completely removed them. Future strategies must address this aspect and counter it by strengthening of tax administration and creation of effective deterrence against evasion of indirect taxes.

One of the main thrust in indirect tax administration can be the collection of more data and creation of greater data-processing capacity that can then be integrated with other data and help multiply the system's sensitivity in flagging potential evaders and initiating action against them.

As an example, for curtailing TBML, there should be institutional arrangement for examining cases of mismatch between export and corresponding import data, as done by the Data Analysis and Research for Trade Transparency System (DARTTS) of US Customs. Indian Customs can consider setting up a trade transparency unit (TTU) along these lines for which appropriate legal framework may be introduced. Existing Customs Cooperation Agreements mostly provide for mutual administrative assistance in individual cases under investigation. These agreements should have institutional arrangement for exchange of harmonised system of nomenclature (HSN) chapter-wise data of export and import. Similar arrangements can be made for preferential trade agreements (PTAs) and free trade agreements (FTAs).

C.10 Strengthening of FIU-IND: Further strengthening of the FIU will remain an important part of the overall strategy for creating stronger deterrence against generation of unaccounted wealth and its use in various legal and illegal activities. The FIU-IND has already initiated project FINnet (financial intelligence network) so as to adopt industry best practices and appropriate technology to collect, analyse and disseminate valuable financial information for combating money laundering and related crimes. Project FINnet would greatly enhance efficiency and effectiveness in the FIU-IND's core function of collection, analysis, and dissemination of financial information. The contract with the system integrator was signed in February 2010 and the new technical infrastructure is being rolled out. Such efforts will need to be expanded further.

The development and identification of 88 red flag indicators by a Working Group of the representatives of the Indian Banks' Association (IBA), the Bank of India, and FIU-IND has been a major development in the supervision of financial activities. These red flags, which are to be shared with the reporting entities and regulators, are currently in the process of being implemented for generation of alerts.

C.11 Strengthening of CEIB: Upgradation of IT capability and networking for the CEIB to effectively fulfil its primary role of collation, analysis, and dissemination of intelligence and information to the concerned agencies needs to be undertaken. A decision was taken at the meeting of the Economic Intelligence Council chaired by the Hon'ble Finance Minister to set up a multidisciplinary school of economic intelligence for developing capacity building in the area of the economic intelligence. Steps are being taken to set up the school and determine its curriculum.

C.12 Strengthening of Other Institutions: The Directorate of Revenue Intelligence and Enforcement Directorate can be further strengthened to play an important role in the coordinated functioning of various monitoring agencies. Capacity building of the functionaries, use of updated technology, and integrated utilisation of databases may be important steps towards achieving this end.

C.13 Other Steps to Curb Generation of Black Money within India: There is a need to recognise serious and habitual tax evasion as crime and implement a strict regime of fiscal and penal consequences to provide effective deterrence against habitual tax evasion. The prosecution mechanism in the income tax department needs to be strengthened and direct tax laws and procedures streamlined. Review of the system of legal advice in prosecution matters and putting in place effective machinery to implement prosecution provisions, including a witness protection programme, are areas that also need to be looked into. The income tax department has already initiated action in all these directions.

The law and procedures for collecting and reporting of information, including third-party information both from domestic and international sources, and its effective utilization, also need to be revamped. Mechanisms for verification of information need to be strengthened. Effective data mining of vast information collected needs to be put in place so that any possible case of non-disclosure or tax evasion is red-flagged and reported and immediate action taken to collect the due taxes and prosecute tax offenders in serious and habitual cases.

The joint task force (JTF) approach needs to be adopted for dealing with serious cases of corruption, tax frauds, terror financing, money-laundering, ponzi/MLM schemes, banking and financial frauds, illegal betting/lottery, etc. The JTF in such cases could consist of all the concerned agencies led by the agency connected with the main infraction of the law.

The effort to tackle the menace of generation and control of black money will need adequate resources to be made available to all the relevant agencies. Emerging areas such as international taxation, transfer pricing, criminal investigation, and exchange of information as well as action thereon, require commensurate resources of manpower, training, technology etc. and necessary budgetary allocation.

D. Supportive Measures

D.1 Creating Public Awareness and Public Support: In a democratic form of government, political will and decisions are often a function of public demand and perception. It is important that citizens are kept in the loop about government strategies, and this paper is one of the steps that the government has specifically adopted in this regard. People must be given to understand how the government views the problem of black money and how it plans to tackle and control it. There is also need to initiate greater public dialogue and debate about the virtues of tax compliance and the menace of black money, while rising above the rhetoric and sincerely attempting to develop a broader understanding of what leads to it and how it can possibly be controlled. It needs to be understood by one and all that state authorities do not possess magic wands with which they can achieve anything that they desire or are directed to achieve.

D.2 Enhancing the Accountability of Auditors: Unlike many developed countries, auditors in India have not been requisitely accountable, resulting in frequent undermining of this important aspect. Apart from recent cases of distortionary corporate governance involving highly reputed firms, cases are detected regularly by the regulatory authorities where the auditors have failed to point out gross violations and even blatant misrepresentations. In the absence of adequate effective provisions, the auditors are hardly ever held accountable for these lapses. Another aspect of this problem is the way in which a firm opts for an auditor in this environment of low accountability and prevalent evasion, since a strict Auditor ready to blow the whistle can hardly expect to thrive amidst competitors, many of whom may be more than willing to cooperate and compromise at different levels. As a result, a very important regulatory tool is virtually losing its role in contributing towards greater compliance. There will be need in future to look into various aspects of the functioning and regulation of the role of auditors and various other professionals verifying the declarations and statements made by firms and ensure that there are adequate safeguards and sufficient accountability of such professionals.

D.3 Protection to Whistleblowers and Witnesses: In India, the law has not been able to provide adequate protection to informants/whistleblowers, nor do government departments have effective witness-protection programmes. As a result, credible information is not forthcoming and witnesses either do not turn up or turn hostile resulting in acquittals in prosecution cases. The DCI in the CBDT has been empowered to run such a programme. Accordingly, a witness-protection law can be considered as an option. Subsequently, witness-protection programmes may need to be implemented by all law enforcement agencies.

D.4 Need to Join International Efforts and Use International Platforms: In a globalized world, where all stakeholders are interdependent, no country can take unilateral measures without adversely impacting its own interests. Thus, in such a scenario, there is greater need to integrate with international efforts and use the international platforms for achieving domestic strategies aimed at curbing black money generation within the country.

India, in earlier summits of the G20, has raised concerns over tax evasion and the difficulties in obtaining necessary information pertaining to past years in cases of tax evasion. Some countries/jurisdictions, unlike most of developed and developing countries, differentiate between 'tax fraud' and 'tax evasion'. For them, while tax fraud is a crime, tax evasion is not. These countries refuse to grant international cooperation and exchange of information regarding tax evasion. This difference in perception assists deliberate concealment of wealth for the purpose of evading tax, something regarded as a crime all over the developed world, and impedes effective exchange of information. There is need to remove this distinction in order to help efforts of government authorities in pursuing tax cheats who have parked funds outside their countries.

India has also been actively advocating making the automatic exchange of information a standard in various International forums including the G20. At present, there is no obligation for countries to exchange information automatically. However, it is necessary to promote automatic exchange of information since this is the best form of exchange of tax information which can promote voluntary compliance and decrease tax evasion. India has requested the G20 countries that they should start exchanging information automatically amongst themselves and then they can give a call and encourage other counties to do so.

Accounting standards can significantly contribute towards greater transparency and help in strengthening deterrence against generation of black money. This is why G20 countries should continue to insist on a 'single set of high quality, global accounting standards' as advocated by it during the Busan Declaration of G20 Finance Ministers. The G20 countries should specifically endorse the idea and implementation of a country-by-country financial reporting standard, which would include the obligation for each multinational company to report in every country in which it operates its relevant particulars including the details of its financial performance, sales, purchases, labour costs, financing costs including facilitation payments, pre-tax profit, tax charges, and book value.

D.5 Need to Fine-tune Relevant Laws and Regulations: There is also need to strengthen the legal framework for regulation. With a changing environment in which those laws are to be implemented, there is urgent need to modify our laws and practices too to make them effective in the prevailing environment. While such efforts are under way in the area of central taxation laws, there are many other laws, related directly or indirectly to the generation of black money that may have to be modified and made more effective. Some of them may be in the nature of paradigm shifts, like the Right to Information Act which has been a major initiative in empowering the citizen and inculcating transparency in the system. Other legislative measures can be aimed at strengthening the deterrence against perpetrators of financial crimes. An example is the recent amendment in the Income Tax Act, whereby the period of limitation for reopening income tax assessments is proposed to be enhanced from the present six years to sixteen years for bringing to tax undisclosed assets held abroad.

Black money cannot be effectively fought unless the

judicial machinery to deal with it is specialized and the trial of offences is expeditious and punishments exemplary. Legal support to various law enforcement agencies should be enhanced. All financial offences should be tried through fast-track special courts. The Ministry of Law may have to take up this issue on priority and make arrangements for setting up fast-track courts all over the country in a time-bound manner. Judicial officers may be provided inputs as required in technical aspects of economic offences.

A professional National Tax Tribunal could be formed to deal with all tax litigation. It has also been suggested that for criminal trial of economic offences, the High Courts may consider setting up exclusive economic offences courts with special summary procedure. Under economic laws, different punishments are prescribed for different offences. Minimum punishments should also be prescribed for economic offences for greater deterrence. Enhanced punishment, at par with other serious economic offences, is likely to provide more effective deterrence against corruption.

D.6 Strengthening of Social Values: The fight against the menace of black money needs to be fought simultaneously at ethical, socioeconomic, and administrative levels. At ethical level, we have to reinforce value/moral education in the school curriculum and build good citizens, particularly highlighting the ills of tax evasion and black money. At socio-economic level, the thrust of public policy should be to discourage conspicuous and wasteful consumption/expenditure, encourage savings, frugality and simplicity, and reduce the gap between the rich and the poor.

Strategies for Curbing Generation of Black Money through Illegal or Criminal Activities

Illegal and criminal activities are an equally significant source of black money generation and curbing them is as an equally important priority of the government. Since many of these activities fall within the ambit of law and order issues, they lie primarily in the domain of state governments. Without undermining the role of the central government, it can be said that strategies for curbing these illegal activities require active participation of state governments, making it even more important that a broader national consensus is achieved in these areas and all political stakeholders commit themselves to pursuing these strategies.

A. Organised Crime: Organised crime, wherever and whenever it exists, lead to profiteering and accumulation of wealth that cannot be reported, thereby generating black money. Such black money is either laundered and brought back into the accountable economy or is taken out of the country or remains within the country, where it may get invested in benami properties, both tangible and intangible in nature. Organised crime can exist in many areas and can often get mixed up with unreported legitimate activities in vulnerable sectors. For example, a property dealer resorting to forceful illegal eviction of tenants can be indulging in both legitimate and illegitimate activities to generate black money. Strict action by state governments is necessary to curb these crimes.

B. Corruption: Today corruption is perceived as one of the major challenges faced by the country, and this government is fully committed to countering it. While a detailed discussion touching on all the factors that lead to corruption and the wider reforms of policies and their execution may be outside the scope of this paper, it can be stated that curbing corruption also requires multi-pronged strategies consisting of both broader reforms as well as more focused capacity building of institutions that are assigned the responsibility of preventing it.

The government has introduced the Public Procurement Bill, 2012. This Bill intends to regulate public procurement by all ministries and central government departments. It aims at ensuring transparency, fair and equitable treatment of bidders, promoting competition, and enhancing efficiency and economy in the public procurement process.

Social-sector schemes involving huge public expenditure under various programmes reportedly suffer from manipulations and leakages. Direct transfers to the accounts of beneficiaries can provide a solution, as they would prevent manipulations like bogus muster rolls. While efforts such as the UID and direct transfer of subsidies will stop leakages in some sectors, in other sectors the problem will have to be addressed differently.

Institutions of the Lok Pal and Lokayukta need to be put in place at the earliest, in the centre and states respectively, to expedite investigations into cases of corruption and bring the guilty to justice. The legislative step in respect of the Lok Pal has already been taken and the bill is under the consideration of the Parliament. In addition, other bills in this context that are pending with the Parliament for enactment are Public Interest Disclosure and Protection to Persons Making the Disclosure Bill, 2010 (Whistleblowers' Bill), Judicial Standards and Accountability Bill, 2010 and Citizens' Grievance Redressal Bill, 2010.

C. Other Criminal Activities that lead to Significant Black Money: There are many illegal activities and crimes that lead to significant income that cannot be reported due to the illegal nature of the activities generating it. These include counterfeit currency, drug trade, and terrorism. Each one of them can be a major source of black money generation and controlling them is one of the great challenges before society. It requires all agencies of both the central and the state governments to actively draw out long-term strategies to bring them to a halt.

Strategies for Repatriation of Black Money Stashed Abroad and Issues Related to Confidentiality of Information

A. Repatriation of Black Money Stashed Abroad: The Government of India has repeatedly expressed its commitment to bringing back black money stashed abroad by Indian citizens. However, it is a goal that cannot be achieved unilaterally by government action. It requires coordination and cooperation of the other country. To achieve this end, the government has been rigorously working to evolve an environment and create legal mechanisms for such cooperation through global consensus and specific bilateral treaties. The network of DTAAs and TIEAs, which has been highlighted in Chapter 4, is a major step in this direction. However, these DTAAs/TIEAs do not have provisions for repatriation of undisclosed assets. There are limited provisions in some of the existing laws.

However, there is no international consensus to have mechanism for repatriation of undisclosed assets located abroad. Without international consensus on this issue it is difficult to implement domestic law on repatriation of assets located abroad. The only exception is the provision under the United Nations Convention against Corruption (UNCAC) where, if it is established that the undisclosed asset represents corruption money, it can be seized and repatriated. India has ratified the UNCAC on 9th May 2012 and thus in cases of corruption, it will be an effective tool for repatriation of assets located abroad.

The Restitution of Illegal Assets Act, 2011, passed by Swiss Parliament in October 2010, provides for freezing, forfeiture and restitution of politically exposed persons, or their associates, where a request made under MLAT cannot produce a result due to failure of state structures in the requesting state. The failure of state structure would be in cases where the requesting state cannot satisfy the requirements of MLATs owing to the total or substantial collapse, or the unavailability of its national judicial system. Since India has a well-functioning judicial system as also a well-functioning MLAT with Switzerland, we do not need to take recourse to this Act.

Under the Income Tax Act, tax, penal interest, and penalty (from 100 percent to 300 percent of the tax evaded) is levied whenever there is information about undisclosed assets located abroad. In most cases this is equivalent to or more than 100 percent of value of the undisclosed asset. The tax liability (including penalty) can then be recovered from Indian assets. If the tax liability cannot be recovered from Indian assets, assistance of the other country (where the undisclosed asset is located), can be taken if in the DTAA there is a provision for assistance in tax collection. This provision exists in 30 of India's 82 DTAAs (Norway, Botswana, Romania, Denmark, Poland, Turkmenistan, Kazakhstan, Sweden, South Africa, Belarus, Trinidad and Tobago, Jordan, Czech Republic, Morocco, Portuguese Republic, Belgium, Kyrgyz Republic, Bangladesh, Ukraine, Uganda, Sudan, Armenia, Iceland, Tajikistan, Luxembourg, Qatar, Mexico, Uruguay, Mozambique, and Georgia). Steps are being taken to include this provision in other DTAAs as well.

India has ratified the Multilateral Convention on Mutual Administrative Assistance in Tax Matters on 2nd February 2012 and it will be in force from 1st June 2012. This Convention provides for assistance in tax collection from countries that are parties to the Convention (provided they have not placed any reservation on this type of assistance) and thus India will become better equipped to repatriate the money from these countries to the extent of tax liability.

Stolen Assets Recovery (StAR) is a partnership between the World Bank Group and UNODC (United Nations Office on Drugs and Crime) that supports international efforts to end safe havens for corrupt funds. Towards this end, it brings together governments' regulatory authorities, financial institutions, and civil society for collective responsibility and action for the deterrence, detection, and recovery of stolen assets. India has taken steps to associate itself with the StAR initiative.

Within this legal framework, the Indian government has been taking steps to recover illegal money that has been stashed abroad. The Government will need to expand the legal framework of DTAAs and TIEAs as in last few years it has been a very useful source of information. Government will also need to sustain its efforts to obtain such information and take strict follow-up action against tax evaders. Building global consensus on assistance on repatriation of money in tax-evasion cases would facilitate the process.

B. Voluntary Disclosure Schemes and Tax Recovery: One of the options suggested for bringing back black money stashed overseas is scheme for voluntary disclosure of such deposits. This option has been successfully adopted by some countries (USA, UK, France, Germany, etc.). In these schemes, only partial benefits in the form of immunity from prosecution were made available in lieu of voluntary disclosure, as taxes along with lump sum interest and penalty has to be paid. In the past, India has also opted for voluntary disclosure schemes. A similar scheme, targeted at black money stashed abroad can be a one time option, in view of the increasing capacity of tax administration to access information from foreign jurisdiction. However, these schemes have also been criticized for creating future expectations of similar schemes and resultant moral hazard. In recent years, the general public sentiment is also perceived to be against giving any immunity to tax evaders who have parked their money outside India. While such schemes help in recovering some of the lost tax revenue, their overall feasibility needs to be assessed in this background.

A gold deposit scheme has also been suggested from some quarters in this regard which essentially provides that if the depositors part with gold now, they will get it back as gold. This may also carry a nominal rate of return and should be transferable so as to be used as collateral for sale. The most important part of the scheme is that there should be complete tax immunity if the holders come forward to make the deposit and the depositors ought not to be asked where they get the gold from. However, the issue of complete tax immunity needs to be examined in light of other policy objectives.

C. Agreement between Countries for Revenue Sharing: There is administrative agreement between the UK and

Switzerland which allows Switzerland to share taxes with the UK on accounts of UK citizens in Swiss Bank. In this regard, it may be noted that on 24th August 2011, UK and Switzerland have initialled a tax agreement in respect of capital income derived by UK residents from assets in Switzerland. The agreement facilitates the levying of tax by the UK on such income in two ways:

1. A retrospective charge in respect of accounts that were operative as on 31st December 2010 and on 31st May 2013; and
2. A tax charge on any future income.

In terms of the retrospective tax charge, the UK resident will be charged tax either as a one-off lump-sum payment (tax rate between 19 and 34 percent of the value of assets) without disclosure of name; or s/he can allow disclosure of her/his account and then be taxed in accordance with the law. The tax charge on future income will be subjected to a final withholding tax of 27 percent (for capital gains) and 48 percent (for investment income). This is basically a revenue-sharing agreement. The agreement is expected to enter into force at the end of 2013. Similar revenue-sharing agreements have also been made between Germany and Switzerland and Austria and Switzerland.

India has already taken up this issue with Switzerland. However, it needs to assess the costs and likely benefits of the step before taking any policy decision. It may be seen that the agreement between the UK and Switzerland is more of a revenue-sharing model which allows revenue sharing at the cost of disclosing identity. The disclosure of name is allowed only when the UK resident, holding assets in Switzerland, volunteers to disclose her/his name or when UK tax authorities make a request after establishing foreseeable relevance criteria.

Thus, India will have to take a decision first as to whether such type of agreement will meet its national objective where it can get an opportunity to share taxes with the Swiss government on assets held by Indian residents in Switzerland without learning the identity of the defaulting Indian residents. The Government of India looks forward to discussion on this important issue within and outside parliament before taking any further steps.

D. Confidentiality of Information under DTAAs/TIEAs: The Government is bound by the treaty provisions under which information is received. As per the international standard, tax information exchanged under DTAAs/TIEAs is protected by the confidentiality clause of the respective DTAA/TIEA under which information is received. The confidentiality provisions of these DTAAs/TIEAs generally allow disclosure or use of information only for tax purposes. India has been trying to renegotiate its DTAAs or conclude new DTAAs/TIEAs by excluding the confidentiality clause but has not met with much success.

While some countries have agreed to include a provision that allows sharing of information with other law enforcement agencies subject to fulfilment of certain conditions they have generally refused to accept India's request to completely eliminate the confidentiality provisions, as they strongly feel that the information should not be made public until the tax case comes up before a court. These countries insist on such confidentiality in order to protect human rights which are also recognised in India.

For example, if we receive information about 100 Indians having bank accounts abroad from a country, it does not prove automatically that all these 100 accounts represent black money of Indian citizens stashed aboard. There may be cases where the account holder may be an NRI who is not assessed to tax in India with respect to those sums or the sum deposited may already have been disclosed to the Income Tax Department. It is only after enquiry and completion of assessment that one can say for sure whether the amount deposited in the foreign bank account represents black money of an Indian citizen stashed abroad.

In order to ensure that there is no delay in these names

becoming public after completion of assessment, the government has taken a view that in cases where any undisclosed overseas asset is detected (including undisclosed foreign bank accounts) one need not wait for disposal of first appeal or imposition of penalty in order to launch prosecution. Accordingly, prosecution was launched in 17 cases immediately after completion of assessments based on information received from German authorities about Indians having bank account in LGT banks and these 17 names have become public on initiating prosecution. Similar procedure can be followed in other cases where undisclosed overseas assets have been detected.

Further, India is also under international obligation to maintain the confidentiality of the information received under DTAAs/TIEAs. In this context, it is subject to the peer review process of all the countries being undertaken by the Global Forum on Transparency and Exchange of Information for Tax Purposes. India is a vice chair of the Peer Review Group of the Global Forum.

The Peer Review Group is assessing all the countries against a set of references. One of the terms of reference clearly mandates confidentiality of information as well as correspondences between competent authorities. Any breach of the confidentiality clause will not only affect India's rating in its peer review but also its international image and give a signal that India is not committed to its international obligations. This may seriously put at risk India's efforts to get similar information from other countries in the future. Thus public disclosure of information received from Germany, France, or other countries need to be used in a way that is in accordance with India's international obligations and do not jeopardise any future efforts in this regard.

There is another related question, namely how the treaty with France is relevant for not disclosing the names of Indians having accounts in Swiss banks. Under the DTAA, countries are obliged to exchange information available within their country if it leads to detection of tax evasion and it does not matter from which country the information has been sourced. Hence, France is under obligation to exchange information with India under the India-France DTAA if it is holding information about Indian citizens' bank accounts which is likely to lead to detection of tax evasion even if the bank accounts are located in a third country. Further, it is also an international standard that the supplying state should exchange information even if it does not have domestic interest in it.

This document makes a serious attempt at putting together a framework for addressing the issue of black money, its generation and strategies for recovering illicit wealth. It is expected that this document would provide a basis for a more informed public debate on the subject. The complexity of the factors that underline the problem necessitates a broad based consensus across the political and institutional divide as well as between governments at different levels. The success in forging a consensus on the policy modalities to regulate and eventually eradicating this scourge will go a long way in making the country more equitable and efficient for facilitating human enterprise.

End Notes

1. Laffer curve is a relationship between government revenue raised by taxation and all possible rates of taxation.
2. RuPay is the Indian domestic card payment network being set up by National Payments Corporation of India (NPCI).

Appendix 2

Direct Taxes Enquiry Committee (Chairman: Justice K.N. Wanchoo), 1971

Government of India, Ministry of Finance

Extracts on Black Money and Tax Evasion

Note: *The Direct Taxes Enquiry Committee (DTEC) was constituted by Government of India on March 2, 1970. The Committee was asked to:*

(a) recommend concrete and effective measures:

(i) to unearth black money and prevent its proliferation through further evasion;

(ii) to check avoidance of tax through various legal devices, including the formation of trusts; and

(iii) to reduce tax arrears.

(b) examine various exemptions allowed by the Tax Laws with a view to their modification, curtailment, or withdrawal.

(c) indicate the manner in which tax assessment and administration may be improved for giving effect to all its recommendations.

Composition of the Committee

K.N. Wanchoo	Chairman
M.P. Chitale	Member
S. Prakash Chopra	Member
P.C. Padhi	Member
D.K. Rangnekar	Member
S. Narayan	Secretary

The Committee considered, inter alia, the problem of tax evasion and established the income on which tax was evaded for 1968-69 at a figure of ₹ 1,400 crore. The amount of tax evasion for the same year was put at ₹ 470 crore [pp. 7-8 of the Report].

The Committee suggested various measures to fight the evil of tax evasion. Some of the measures suggested were as follows:

1. *Reduction in tax rates.*
2. *Minimisation of controls and licences.*
3. *Regulation of donations to political parties.*
4. *Creating confidence among small taxpayers.*
5. *Substitution of sales tax by excise duty.*
6. *Vigorous prosecution policy.*
7. *Compulsory maintenance of accounts.*

To give effect to the recommendations made by the Committee, the Government enacted the Taxation Laws (Amendment) Act, 1975. This Act, inter alia, provided stringent punishment for tax evaders. In cases where tax evasion exceeded ₹ 1 lakh or prosecution was for the second or subsequent offence, the maximum punishment prescribed was seven years rigorous imprisonment. Also, the discretionary powers to courts to award monetary punishment as an alternative to imprisonment or to reduce the term of imprisonment less than the minimum period, was withdrawn.

The Report of DTEC was a milestone in the area of income tax rates. The Committee made a number of far-reaching suggestions for unearthing black money, preventing evasion and avoidance of taxes, and reducing arrears. One important recommendation of the Committee related to reduction in the rates of direct taxes which in its view were mainly responsible for tax evasion because they made tax evasion profitable and attractive. The rates of individual income tax were quite high till the year 1973-74. However, pursuant to the recommendations of the DTEC, the Government initiated a series of rate reductions in individual income tax. The rate of tax was reduced from 97.7 percent in 1973-74 to 77 percent in 1974-75, and further down to 66 percent in 1976-77. It is noteworthy that DTEC had recommended a maximum marginal rate of 75 percent.

Extracts on Black Money and Tax Evasion

The term 'black money' not only stands for money earned by violating legal provisions—even social conscience—but also suggests that such money is kept secret and not accounted for.

Today, the term 'black money' is generally used to denote unaccounted money or concealed income and/or undisclosed wealth, as well as money involved in transactions wholly or partly suppressed.

Tax evasion and black money are closely and inextricably inter-linked. While tax evasion leads to the creation of black money, the black money utilised secretively in business for earning more income inevitably leads to tax evasion.

The effect of 'black money' on the economy of the country cannot but be described as disastrous. Today, the country is seriously handicapped in its endeavour to march forward, when the resources needed for development are not adequately forthcoming for the reasons that business is carried on in the 'black'.

Black money is like a cancerous growth in the country's economy which, if not checked in time, is sure to lead to its ruination.

Extent of Black Money and Tax Evasion

Research work on tax evasion in this country is extremely limited; also, attempts to estimate and study tax evasion suffer from some basic infirmities owing to the insufficiency or non-availability of reliable data. Unless a detailed break-down of the total assessed income generated in each year is available, it is difficult to make a scientific study of the trend of tax evasion.

The conclusion of this study is that the income which escaped tax for 1961-62 would be of the order of ₹ 811 crore.

Applying the ratio of evaded income to the assessable non-salary income of 1961-62, to the assessable non-salary income of 1965-66, the evaded income for 1965-66 works out to ₹ 1,216 crore.

These estimates have, however, to be qualified for certain reasons. Even after taking all these limitations into account and after making rough adjustments on the basis of information available, the estimated income on which tax has been evaded would probably be ₹ 700 crore and ₹ 1,000 crore for the year 1961-62 and 1965-66 respectively. Projecting this estimate further to 1968-69 on the basis of the percentage of increase in the national income from 1961-62 to 1968-69 (during which period the national income increased nearly by 100 percent), the income on which tax was evaded for 1968-69 can be estimated at a figure of ₹ 1,400 crore.

The extent of income tax evaded during 1968-69 would be of the order of ₹ 470 crore, being one-third of ₹ 1,400 crore. The money value of deals involving black money may, therefore, be not less than ₹ 7,000 crore for 1968-69. This is, however, only a guesstimate based on certain assumptions about which substantial difference of opinion exists for want of adequate data.

The tax-evaded income is not all lying hoarded which can be seized by the authorities; much of it has been either converted into assets or spent away in consumption or else is in circulation in undisclosed business dealings.

Avenues for Black Money

Black money is found widely used for conducting concealed business transactions, smuggling gold and luxury articles, purchasing illegally quotas and licences at premia, financing secret commissions, giving donations to political parties, acquiring assets in benami names, etc. Behind the vulgar display of wealth which is evidenced by ostentatious living and lavish expenditure on weddings, festivals, etc., is this scourge of black money.

Causes of Tax Evasion, Creation of Black Money and its Proliferation

1. High rates of taxation under the direct tax laws.
2. Economy of shortages and consequent controls and licences.
3. Donations to political parties.
4. Corrupt business practices.
5. Ceilings on, and disallowance of, business expenses.
6. High rates of sales-tax and other levies.
7. Ineffective enforcement of tax laws.
8. Deterioration in moral standards.

Measures for Unearthing Black Money

Voluntary Disclosure Scheme: A voluntary disclosure scheme is an extraordinary measure, meant for abnormal situations such as after a war or at a time of national crisis. Resorting to such a measure during normal times, and that too frequently, would only shake the confidence of the honest taxpayers in the capacity of the Government to deal with the law breakers and would invite contempt for its enforcement machinery. Any more disclosure schemes would not only fail to achieve the intended purpose of unearthing black money but would have deleterious effect on the level of compliance among the tax-paying public and on the morale of the administration. The idea of introduction of any general scheme of disclosure either now or in the future is, therefore, strongly opposed.

Settlement Machinery: In the administration of fiscal laws a rigid attitude would not only inhibit a one-time tax-evader or an unintending defaulter from making a clean breast of his affairs, but would also unnecessarily strain the investigational resources of the Department in cases of doubtful benefit to revenue, while needlessly proliferating litigation and holding up collections. There should, therefore, be a provision in a law for a settlement with the taxpayer at any stage of the proceedings.

To ensure that settlements are fair, prompt and independent, they may be entrusted to a separate body within the Department, to be called the Direct Taxes Settlement Tribunal. Its members should be given the same status and emoluments as the members of the Central Board of Direct Taxes.

Any taxpayer will be entitled to move a petition before the Tribunal for settlement of his liability under the direct tax laws. However, the Tribunal will proceed with the petition filed by a taxpayer only if the Department raises no objection to its being so entertained. Once a case is admitted for adjudication, the Tribunal will have exclusive jurisdiction over it and it will no longer be open to the taxpayer to withdraw the petition. The Tribunal's award will be binding both on the petitioner and on the Department.

It is of paramount importance that only persons who are known for their integrity and high sense of justice and fairness are selected for appointment on the Tribunal.

Bearer Bonds: The bearer bond scheme is a poor substitute even for a discloser scheme. The so called benefits claimed for the bearer bond schemes are illusory.

Swiss Type Bank Accounts: It is not worthwhile to experiment with the Swiss type of bank accounts in India.

Canalising Black Money into Certain Specified Fields: Sponsoring official schemes for canalising black money into specified social and other fields of activity will not be desirable.

Searches and Seizures: The power of search under the Income Tax Act is potent instrument in the hands of the Department of provide direct and clinching evidence about tax evasion and the existence of black money. The Department should make an increasing use of its powers of search and seizure in appropriate cases.

The following changes are recommended so as to render this instrument more effective:

(a) A commissioner of income tax should have power to

authorise search and seizure, irrespective of whether the tax payer is assessed in his jurisdiction or not.

(b) The power of authorising searches and seizures should be available to the inspective assistant commissioners as well.

(c) The existing powers of search under the Income Tax Act should be extended to cover persons, vehicles and vessels.

(d) The period for making an order under Section 132(5) of the Income Tax Act, 1961, may be extended from the present ninety days to one hundred and eighty days.

(e) The law may be amended to permit retention of seized assets in order to meet the liability of interest and penalty, in addition to the tax, that may become due on the estimated undisclosed income.

(f) Section 132(8) of the Income Tax Act, 1961, may be amended to provide that the 'authorised officer' and/or the income tax officer having jurisdiction over the case may apply for retention of the seized material beyond the period of 180 days.

Similarly, Section 132(9) of the Income Tax Act, 1961, which contemplates copies, etc., of seized documents being made in the presence of the 'authorised officer', or any other person empowered by him in this behalf, may be suitably amended.

(g) The law may be amended to raise a presumption to the effect that, unless proved to the contrary by the assessee, the assets which are seized in the course of a search will be deemed to represent the concealed income and wealth of the previous year/valuation date immediately preceding the date of search.

(h) It is often difficult for the Department to get independent evidence to prove that the assets, account books and documents found at the assessee's premises belong to him and relate to his affairs. The law may, therefore, be amended to provide a rebuttable presumption both for estimating the undisclosed income and also for prosecution of an assessee or an abettor.

The Department should ensure that the actions of its officers in the matter of searches and seizures do not leave any room for complaint, and whenever any officer is found, in his misplaced enthusiasm, to err and overstep the limits of reasonableness, he should be promptly and adequately dealt with. Moreover, it is of paramount importance that the assessments in cases where seizures have been made in the course of searches are finalised expeditiously and are not allowed to drag on unnecessarily.

The power of search, if it is to be purposeful, must be backed by a far better system of intelligence than what obtains to day. The provision empowering searches and seizures can act as a deterrent only if really big tax evaders are uncovered and the exercise of this power is not confined to relatively small and less important assesses.

Measures to Fight Tax Evasion

Reduction in Tax Rates: Prevalence of high tax rates is the first and for most reason for tax evasion, because this is what makes the evasion so profitable and attractive in spite of the attendant risks.

If public conscience is to be aroused against tax evasion and if tax evaders are to be ostracised by the society at large, the public needs to be convinced that tax evasion is antisocial. This objective is difficult to achieve so long as the marginal rates of taxation are confiscatory.

The high rats of taxation create a psychological barrier to greater effort and undermine the capacity and the will to save and invest.

The present high level of taxation leaves the Government with little scope for manoeuvrability for raising additional resources in times of emergency.

The maximum marginal rate of income tax, including surcharge, should be brought down from its present level of 97.75 percent to 75 percent. Some reduction in tax rates should also be given at the middle and lower levels. In order to create an impact, the reduction in the rates of taxation should be at one stroke.

The beneficial result of the measure recommended will catch up and more than offset any immediate fall in the revenues.

Minimisation of Controls and Licences: A committee of experts should be appointed to enquire into the utility of all existing controls, licensing and permit systems, and suggest elimination of such of these as are no longer considered necessary. This committee may also suggest changes in law and procedures so as to ensure that the controls which are absolutely essential for the health of the economy are administered more effectively and with the least harassment to the public.

Regulation of Donations to Political Parties: There is need to keep political institutions free of corruption. Removal of the ban on donations by companies to political parties is, therefore, not favoured. Nevertheless, it is an accepted fact of life that in a democratic set-up, political parties have to spend considerable sums of money and that large sums are required for elections. As in West Germany and Japan, in our country also, the Government should finance political parties.

Reasonable grants-in-aid should be given by the Government to national political parties and suitable criteria should be evolved for recognizing such parties and determining the extent of grant-in-aid to each of them. For according recognition to a political party for this purpose, it should be necessary, *inter alia,* that it is registered under the Societies Registration Act, 1860 and its yearly accounts are audited and published within a prescribed time. Irrespective of the decision of Government on the question of financing political parties, the parties may be required to get their accounts audited and published annually.

Donations by taxpayers, other than companies, to recognised political parties should be allowed as a deduction from the gross total income subject to certain restrictions. The maximum amount eligible for deduction on account of donations to political parties should be 10 percent of the gross total income, subject to a ceiling of rupees ten thousand. The deduction to be allowed should be 50 percent of the qualifying amount of the donation.

Creating Confidence among Small Taxpayers: The practice of being to meticulous in small cases, where no worthwhile revenue is involved, has done much to damage the image of the Department in the public eye. The initiative for undoing the danger lies with the Department.

The instructions issued by the Central Board of Direct Taxes on the new procedure for making assessments in small income cases make a bold departure from the past and are likely to achieve more significant results than the earlier small income scheme. While the general principles underlying these instructions are broadly approved, there is no reason why assesses in certain income groups at some places should be given a preferential treatment by having their returns accepted under Section 143(1), whereas elsewhere assesses in these income groups will have to face annual scrutiny. The basic criteria for selecting cases for annual scrutiny should be uniform throughout the country.

The work may be so programmed and the manpower supplemented, if necessary, so as to ensure that at the end of each financial year the carry over of work should not be more than what can be disposed of the next four months.

Notwithstanding the proposed discontinuance of issuing notice under Section 139(2) of the Income Tax Act in every case, the Department should mail the return forms together with instructions for filling them to all existing taxpayers on the General Index Registers in the first week of May every year.

Allowance of Certain Business Expenses: Entertainment expenditure which is incurred primarily for the furtherance of the taxpayer's business and is directly related to its active conduct should be allowed to be deducted up to the ceilings prescribed under Section 37 (2A) of the Income Tax Act, 1961.

The exception contained in the second proviso to Section 37(4) of Income Tax Act, 1961 should be made applicable to guest houses maintained in the nature of transit houses for employees on duty, provided the stay is temporary and rent is charged. Whether no rent is charged, the daily allowance admissible to the employee should be restricted on the same lines as for Government servants.

Changes in Penal Provisions: Penalty serves its purpose only so long a sit is within reasonable limit. Once it crosses that limit, it is more likely to increase the rigidity of the taxpayer's recalcitrance than to reform him.

A penalty based on income instead of tax hits the smaller taxpayers more harshly.

The quantum of penalty imposable for concealment of income should be with reference to the tax sought to be evaded, instead of the income concealed. Moreover, the minimum penalty imposable for concealment of income should be the amount of tax sought to be evaded and the maximum penalty imposable should be fixed at twice the said amount. It may also be clarified that 'tax sough to be evaded' in this context means the difference between the tax determined in respect of total income assessed and the tax that would have been payable had the income other than the concealed income been the total income.

In case where the concealed income is to be set off against losses incurred by an assessee under other heads of income or against losses brought forward from earlier years, and the total income thus gets reduced to a figure smaller than the concealed income or even to a minus figure, the tax sought to be evaded should be calculated as if the concealed income were the total income.

Explanation to Section 271(1)(c) of the Income Tax Act, 1961 and also Explanation 1 to Section 18(1)(c) of the Wealth Tax Act, 1957 may be deleted.

An explanation to Section 271(1) of the Income Tax Act,

1961 may be inserted to clarify that where a taxpayer's explanation in respect of any receipt, deposit, outgoing, or investment is found to be false, the amount represented by such receipt, etc., shall be deemed to be income in respect of which particulars have been concealed or inaccurate particulars have been furnished, with the meaning of Section 271(1)(c) of the Income Tax Act, 1961.

Law should be amended to provide that where intangible additions made in earlier years are cited by an assessee as the source of his funds, assets, etc., in a subsequent year, the said funds, assets, etc., would be deemed to represent the assessee's income, particulars in respect of which have been concealed within the meaning of Section 27(1)(c) of the Income Tax Act, 1961, and the quantum of penalty would be determined with reference to the total income of the said assessment year, which shall be computed for this limited purpose by including the value of such funds, assets, etc., to the extent they are claimed to be out of past intangible additions.

Where an assessee does not file a return of income with the normal period of limitation for completion of assessment, and the income tax officer establishes that he had taxable income, the assessee should be deemed in law to have concealed his total income for the purpose of Section 27(1)(c) of the Act, notwithstanding that he had subsequently, in response to notice under Section 148, filed a return stating his correct income. This will apply only to those who have not hitherto been assessed.

(i) Where return of income is filed under Section 139 (1) of the Income Tax Act, 1961, after the prescribed time-limit but within the period of limitation for completion of assessment, the assessee should be liable to pay only interest at the rate of 1 percent per month on the tax due for the period of delay. There should be no liability for penalty or prosecution.

(ii) Where a return of income is filed beyond the time prescribed under Section 139 (2) or Section 148, but within the time allowed, if any, by the income tax officer, the assessee should be liable to pay interest at the rate of 1 percent per month on the tax due for the period of delay.

(iii) Where a return of income is filed beyond the time prescribed under Section 139 (2) or Section 148 and also beyond the time allowed, if any, by the income tax officer, the assessee should be liable to pay interest at the rate of 1 percent per month and, in addition, penalty at the rate of 1 percent of the tax due for every month during which the default continued.

(iv) Where a person fails to submit a return of income in response to a notice under Section 139 (2) or Section 148 and on assessment his income is found to be above taxable limit, he should be liable to pay interest at the rate of 1 percent per month and, in addition, penalty at the rate of 1 percent of the tax due for every month during which the default continued. He should also be liable to prosecution.

(v) Where a person fails to submit a return as required under Section 139 (1) but submits it in response to a notice under Section 139 (2) or Section 148, he should be liable to pay interest at the rate of 1 percent of the tax due for every month during which the default continued. In the case of a person not hitherto assessed to tax, where the failure has continued beyond the normal period of limitation for completing the assessment under Section 143, he should, in addition to interest, be liable to a penalty under Section 271 (I) (c) as recommended earlier, as also prosecution.

(vi) For the purpose of levy of interest at the rate of 1 percent, the period of delay or default should always be counted from the due date for filing the return of income under Section 139 (I), notwithstanding the extension of time, if any, granted by the income tax officer.

The provisions in clauses (i) and (ii) of Section 18 (1) and clauses (a), (b) and (c) of Section 36 (1) of the Wealth Tax Act, 1957 should be respectively brought in line with the corresponding provisions of the Income Tax Act.

Penalty for concealment of wealth should be restricted to only those cases where there is a total omission to include an asset in the return of net wealth. Further, in order to avoid gross under-valuation, the Government may be given the power to acquire the properties, which are considered to be grossly undervalued, on payment of the value put by the assessee plus 15 percent thereof by way of compensation.

The penalty for concealment of wealth should be linked to the amount of tax sought to be evaded instead of the concealed wealth. The minimum penalty for concealment of wealth under the Wealth Tax Act, 1957 should be equal to the tax sought to be evaded and the maximum penalty should be five times the tax sought to be evaded.

While the present rate of penalty at 2 percent per month prescribed under clause (i) of Section 17 (1) of the Gift Tax Act, 1958 should continue, the ceiling of fifty percent of the tax due should go.

The existing provisions for waiver and reduction of penalties may be deleted and, instead, all the direct tax laws should contain a provision enabling the Commissioner to mitigate or entirely remit any penalty, or stay, or compound any proceedings for recovery thereof, in cases of genuine hardship.

Where a return of income is filed belatedly by an assessee and his income in no year during a period of four years immediately preceding the year exceeded ₹ 15,000, the income tax officer should be under a statutory obligation to consider waiver or reduction of both penalty and interest and should record a note giving reasons for the decision taken by him in the matter.

The present policy of having a statutory minimum for penalties has, on the whole, had salutary effect and it should, therefore, continue.

Vigorous Prosecution Policy: The Department should completely reorient itself to a more vigorous prosecution policy in order to instil fear and wholesome respect for the tax laws in the minds of the taxpayers. Further, where there is a reasonable chance of securing a conviction, the tax dodger should invariably be prosecuted.

While the power to compound offences presently available to the Department under Section 279 (2) of the Income Tax Act, 1961 may continue, it should be used very sparingly. It has also to be emphasized that flagrant cases of tax evasion, particularly of persons in the high income brackets, should be pursued relentlessly.

The definition of 'principal officer' for the purposes of signing of the return should be amended so as to provide that the return of income of a limited company should be signed by the person mainly responsible for the management or administration of the affairs of the company. In other worlds, the liability for signing the return should be fixed primarily on the managing director, failing which on the working director. Similarly, in the case of a partnership, the responsibility to sign the return should rest on the managing partner or the partner in charge of the financial affairs of the firm.

A provision analogous to Section 140 of the Customs Act, 1962 may be incorporated in the Income Tax Act. Further, it should also cover the case of a partner who is really responsible for the tax offence of the firm, although he has not signed the return himself. The choice of person who should be proceeded against should be left to the discretion of the Commissioner of Income tax.

A provision on the lines of Section 7201 of U.S. Internal Revenue Code will be extremely helpful in countering devices of tax evaders. Such a provision should be incorporated in the Indian tax laws also.

Section 18 of the Probation of Offenders Act, 1958 should be suitably amended to include all the direct tax laws among the statutes which are saved from the operation of the Probation of Offenders Act.

There are certain offences, such as those specified in Sections 179 and 180 of the Indian Penal Code, which can be incorporated in the Income tax law itself. The Customs Act, 1962 also contains a comprehensive residuary penalty provision in Section 117, which is to the effect that if any person contravenes any provision of the Customs Act or abets any such contravention or fails to comply with any of its provisions, he shall be liable to a penalty not exceeding ₹ 1,000 in case no express penalty is elsewhere provided for such contravention or failure. Similar provisions should be incorporated in Chapter XXI of the Income Tax Act, 1961 and these contraventions may be made liable to a penalty only.

There is no reason why the Department itself should not be empowered to impose penalties in cases of offences for which monetary fines are prescribed under Section 276 of the Income Tax Act, 1961. Section 276 of the Income Tax Act, 1961, may be deleted from Chapter XXII dealing with 'Offences and Prosecutions' and may be incorporated with suitable amendments in Chapter XXI of the Income Tax Act, 1961, dealing with 'penalties imposable'.

The penalties suggested above should be imposed by offices not below the rank of an inspecting assistant commissioner. The orders imposing penalty may be made appealable to the appellate tribunal by suitably amending Section 253 of the Income Tax Act, 1961.

The law may be suitably amended to exclude the time spent on prosecution, from the institution of the complaint to its final disposal, from the period of limitation prescribed for making an assessment or re-assessment.

Certain magistrates and judges should be specially empowered to try prosecution cases connected with the direct tax laws, so that these cases are heard and decided expeditiously.

For the present, it would be adequate of each commissioner of income tax is provided with a penal of competent lawyers having necessary experience in dealing with criminal cases, so that the complaints are promptly filed and are carefully pursued. The commissioner of income tax should also be provided with expert staff assistance to enable him to give instructions to subordinates and also to follow up every prosecution case to its logical end.

Officers should be given practical training with reference to case studies so that they are fully equipped to work up and process cases for prosecution. They may also be put through special courses in court procedures, mock trails, etc.

Intelligence and Investigation: To cope with the increasing refinement and sophistication of the techniques of tax evasion, there is a need for complete re-orientation in the Department's approach to its methods of intelligence an investigation. The machinery for intelligence and investigation at the command of the Department should also be thoroughly overhauled and streamlined to tackle adequately the menace of tax evasion.

Intelligence and investigation should receive exclusive attention of a senior member of the General Board of Direct Taxes, and the member concerned should be freed of all other work. This member should be designated as Member (Intelligence an Investigation). He should lay down the policy in matters relating to intelligence and investigation, indicate the lines on which efforts of the officer working in these fields should be directed and provide them with overall guidance and supervision. He should also be responsible for: (a) developing expertise generally for handling investigation concerning different trades and industries; (b) collecting and disseminating information regarding commercial and industrial trends, economic malpractices, tax evasion techniques; (c) keeping liaison with the various investigating agencies at Delhi; and (d) giving publicity to the Department's performance in the field of detection of concealments. He should, however, be assisted by two senior officers of the rank of additional commissioners. They may be designated as director (intelligence) and director (investigation). In addition, he should be assisted by a group of Specialists for developing expertise.

The present Directorate of Inspection (Investigation) should be abolished.

As regards the organisational pattern at the Commissioner's level, the ideal position would be to create a separate division for intelligence and investigation under each commissioner of income tax. However, in major cities like Bombay, Calcutta, Delhi and Madras, looking to the workload involved, the intelligence and investigation work should be assigned to commissioner of income tax (Central).

All the commissioners of income tax, whether of Central charges or otherwise, should be assisted by appropriate number of inspecting assistant commissioners of income tax to exclusively look after intelligence and investigation work, the number varying according to the needs of each charge. They may be designated as inspecting assistant commissioners (intelligence) or inspecting assistant commissioner (investigation), according to the work handled by them. The income tax officers working under them will be similarly designated income tax officers (intelligence) and income tax officers (investigation), depending upon the duty allotted.

In the matter of transfer or re-transfer of cases of central circles, the views of the commissioner (central) should alone prevail as it will be his responsibility to work up an adequate number of tax fraud cases every year.

The functions to be assigned to the income tax officer (intelligence) may be divided broadly into three groups. Firstly, one or more income tax officers (intelligence) should be put on the job of procuring general information likely to be useful in detecting concealment. The second group of income tax officers (intelligence) should devote themselves exclusively to specific cases of tax dodgers. The third group of income tax officers (intelligence) will follow up the leads in cases suspected of serious tax fraud, process them for prosecution and pursue them till the stage of conviction. Where an income tax officer (intelligence) has made elaborate enquiries in a particular case over a long period, the jurisdiction for assessment over such a case may also be assigned to him.

The income tax offices (intelligence) should be given the requisite powers under Sections 131 and 133A of Income Tax Act, 1961 to enable them to work up cases effectively. This power should be available to them in respect of all the cases falling within the jurisdiction of the commissioner of income tax under whom they are posted, and not only in respect of assesses, whose cases are specifically allotted to them for assessment.

One staff care should be placed exclusively at the disposal of the Intelligence Wing in each charge.

The Intelligence Wing should be provided with one pick-up each, at least in bigger stations like Delhi, Bombay, Calcutta, Madras, Ahmedabad and Kanpur.

The setting up of an independent constabulary within the income tax department to assist and aid the tax recovery units is being recommended elsewhere. The services of this constabulary can be utilised by the intelligence wing as well.

The officers of the wing in each commissioner's charge, or to begin with at least in bigger charges should be supplied with requisite equipments like magnifying glasses, telephoto cameras, tape-recorders, photostate machines, ultra-violet and infra-red lamps and micro-filming apparatus, etc.

Air travel facility may be extended liberally to all officers in the intelligence Wing, subject to prior approval of the Commissioner of Income tax concerned.

All officers of the intelligence wing should be provided with residential telephones.

To enable the intelligence wing to cope with the enlarged activities as proposed, adequate funds should be placed at its disposal.

The present filed assistance to officers cannot by any standard be considered adequate especially at the level of inspectors. It is essential that the inspectors should frequently *go out suo moto* to scout for information from various sources. The strength of Inspectors should be suitably increased.

It will not be enough merely to have a powerful

intelligence organisation. It has to be accompanied by an equally powerful wing for through and complete investigation of suspect cases so that the fear of the law is instilled into the hearts of the tax dodgers.

In order to improve the quality of investigation, the inspecting assistant commissioners should be drafted for assessment of big cases so that their experience is available for meeting the challenge of the toughest tax evaders. Law may be suitably amended to vest concurrent jurisdiction in the inspecting assistant commissioners (investigation) and income tax officers (investigation).

An officer doing investigation cases should not normally be expected to handle more than 40 to 50 assessments in a year, and where the cases are especially complicated or involve prosecution, the number may be reduced to four or five.

The following factors should be taken into account in deciding transfer of cases to the investigation circles:

(a) The likelihood of establishing tax fraud for successful prosecution.
(b) The necessity of covering all direct taxes and different kinds of tax offences within each charge and also all strata of society and geographic areas.
(c) The necessity of placing emphasis on cases involving racketeers, profiteers, black-marketeers and notorious tax evaders in upper income brackets.
(d) The necessity of giving priority to cases where the available evidence indicates repeated or flagrant violations of law.
(e) The necessity of giving priority to cases where taxpayers have already been convicted for serious economic offences.
(f) The necessity of giving priority to cases where assesses are frittering away or transferring their assets to escape proper liability.
(g) The necessity of laying emphasis on cases having vast

ramifications and involving deftly organised manoeuvres and malpractices.

Normally, it should be possible to complete investigation in any case in three or four years; thereafter, it should be transferred out of the investigation circle. However, if it is desired to retain the case in the investigation circle beyond a period of four years, approval of the members should be obtained.

The officers selected to man the intelligence and investigation jobs should be imparted thorough and intensive training, at the central staff training college, so as to equip them with the necessary expertise for satisfactory performance of their onerous and responsible tasks.

A group of senior and capable officers may be constituted under the Central Board of Direct Taxes to act as specialists for guiding investigation in various important businesses and industries.

The specialists should work under member (intelligence and investigation) and should be selected from among officers who have handled assessments of a particular business of industry over a long period of time and have acquired special ability in that field.

In view of the prevailing large-scale tax evasion it would not be desirable to put an end to the practice of giving monetary inducements to informers. At the same time, it is equally necessary for the Department to ensure that undesirable informers are kept away by prosecuting persons giving false information. Provisions of Section 182 of the Indian Penal Code may be invoked in flagrant cases of informers furnishing false information. The existing reward rules should be made more flexible. While there should be no fixed percentage for payment of rewards, the rules may stipulate that if information furnished by an informer is correct and leads to additional tax, or is otherwise useful in checking tax evasion, the commissioner of income tax and the Central Board of Direct Taxes may, in their discretion, pay rewards up to ₹ 5,000 and ₹ 25,000 respectively.

A specific statutory provision should be made to exempt rewards to informers from tax. This would not only continue the existing inducement available to them but also preserve the secrecy of information and anonymity of the informers.

Instead of constituting a separate cadre, the personnel for the intelligence and investigation division should be selected out of the general cadre on the basis of high integrity, proven ability and special flair for investigation.

The special pay of the income tax officers and the inspecting assistant commissioners put on intelligence and investigation work should be raised to ₹ 200 and ₹ 300 respectively.

The officers working in investigation circles should also be given facilities regarding staff assistance, staff car, air travel and residential telephones.

The Department should widely publicise in newspapers, by way of paid advertisement if necessary, factual details of searches, seizures and prosecutions, without waiting for the result of appeals; and for this purposes, the law may be suitably amended.

Time-limit for Reopening Cases of Tax Evasion: Any change in the law relating to time-limit for reopening of cases is not favoured.

Taxation of Agricultural Income: Agricultural income, which is at present outside the central tax net, offers plenty of scope for camouflaging black money.

There is urgent need for agricultural income being subjected to a uniform tax more or less on par with the tax on other incomes so as to eliminate the scope for evasion of direct taxes imposed by the Union government. Agriculture should also contribute to the national Exchequer in much the same way as other sectors are doing. It is also necessary on grounds of equity and distributive justice.

In the interest of uniformity and stability, the Central Government should assume the power to levy and administer tax on agricultural income.

The Government may choose any of the following courses, as it deems feasible:

(a) The Constitution may be amended to unambiguously empower the Union Government to impose taxes on agricultural income.

(b) The Union Government may impose income tax on agricultural income, provided State Legislatures empower the Union government in this behalf by necessary resolution in accordance with the provisions of Article 252 of the Constitution.

(c) Article 269 of the Constitution may be amended to include taxes on agricultural income in the list of taxes levied and collected by the Union, and the taxes so collected may be assigned to the States in accordance with the procedure outlined therein.

Unexplained Expenditure: A separate legal provision analogous to Sections 69, 69A and 69B, may be made in the Income Tax Act, 1961, which would enable the tax authorities to bring to tax the amount of 'unexplained' expenditure.

Substitution of Sales Tax by Excise Duty: The best way to get over the problem posed by the existing sales tax system would be to replace sales tax levy on various commodities, as far as possible, by additional duty to excise, but in the selection of commodities, care should be taken to minimise the cascading effect on prices. As sales tax will still continue to be levied on some commodities, there should be greater co-ordination between the Income tax authorities and the sales tax authorities in the matter of exchange of information, collection of intelligence about evasion of these taxes and also in taking preventive measures for checking tax evasion.

Compulsory Maintenance of Accounts: A statutory provision may be made requiring maintenance of accounts by all persons in profession, and by businessmen where the income from business is in excess of ₹ 25,000 or turnover or gross receipts are in excess of ₹ 2.5 lakh in any one of the immediately three preceding years. In the case of a new business, the provision will apply, if the income or turnover is likely to exceed these limits.

The law should provide that ledgers and cash books should be preserved for a period of 16 years and other accounts and records for 8 years.

Monetary fines should be provided in the law for failure to maintain accounts in the manner required or to preserve them for the prescribed period. In the initial stages, the department should mount a massive publicity programme to educate the public in this behalf. A mild and conciliatory approach will be needed for some years to come and the penal provisions should be invoked only in flagrant cases of deliberate failure to maintain books or records or to preserve them.

Compulsory Audit of Accounts: A provision may be introduced in the law making presentation of audited accounts mandatory in all cases of business or profession where the sales/turnover/receipts exceed ₹ 5 lakh or the profit before tax exceeds ₹ 50,000. A form of audit report may be prescribed, taking due note of the manner in which documents, records and books are maintained in the non-corporate sector. Auditor's report should include, among other things, pertinent information like the following:

1. Scope of examination—whether full check, test-check or mere reconciliation–in order to satisfy that purchases, sales, income and expenses are properly accounted for and balance sheet is properly drawn up.
2. Nature of security offered for obtaining secured loans. Particulars of security not recorded or accounted for in the books to be stated.
3. Computation of admissible allowance by way of depreciation.
4. Brief particulars of expenditure on entertainment, advertisement, guest house, etc., and the amount, if any, disallowable under Section 37 of the Income Tax Act, 1961.

5. Particulars of expenses in respect of which payments have been made to directors, partners or persons substantially interested in the concern and their relatives. The amount, if any, not deductible under Sections 40 and 40A of the Income Tax Act, 1961.
6. Particulars of amounts, if any, chargeable as profits under Section 41 of the Income Tax Act, 1961.
7. Particulars of payments in respect of which income tax has not been deducted at source and paid in accordance with the requirements of Sections 192-200 of the Income Tax Act, 1961.

The Government may also, in due course, evolve a proforma of information to be furnished by the auditors which would facilitate completion of assessments.

Permanent Account Number: The absence of a uniform system of indexing all taxpayers in the country on a permanent basis has to some extent been responsible for the difficulties experiences by the department in tackling tax evasion. It has prevented proper linking of information expeditiously to the assessee to whom it relates and has also resulted in the records and the accounts of the taxpayers not being properly maintained. There is no gainsaying the fact that both the taxpayers and the department will stand to benefit by the introduction of a system of permanent account numbers.

The length of the code should be minimal. Unduly long codes are likely to lead to serious errors in reproduction, particularly in the existing manual system. The system should, however, be capable of covering the entire Section of the population which it is intended to cover and also provide sufficient room for expansion over the projected useful life of the code. The code should be permanently assigned to an entity to provide historical continuity and to facilitate data processing operations. The code should have a fixed number of characters so that, while being suitable for manual processing, it could be adopted without change when machine processing is widely introduced.

The code to be adopted for taxpayer identification should be numeric. The adoption of an assigned numeric code with a uniform number of digits is, therefore, recommended. The addition of a checking code to the permanent account number is not favoured.

Numbers should be allotted, at any rate in the initial stage, only to the taxpayers who are already on the registers of the department or who come on to the registers subsequently. There should of course be a provision to enable any one desirous of obtaining an account number to do so. Perhaps number could also be allotted to all those who were on the registers of the Department till recently before, the exemption limit was raised to ₹ 5,000.

Account numbers once allotted should remain unchanged as long as the entity continues to exist as such.

It will be necessary to have an additional code, a 'Records Locator Code', to help locate the records of a taxpayer when the case is transferred from one circle to another after the permanent account number has been allotted. To avoid confusion with the permanent numeric code, this records locator code may be a short alphabetic code. It will not be a part of the permanent code and will not in any way vitiate its permanent character.

Though the permanent account number could be put to a variety of uses, it will be most used by the income tax department and as such it will only be appropriate if the requisite legislation is incorporated in the Income Tax Act itself.

Apart from fulfilling its role of a permanent, identifying number for record keeping, the permanent account number can also serve as an effective tool for combating tax evasion detecting fraud and spotting new assesses, if legal provisions are introduced requiring persons to quote on the documents relating to specified transactions, their own account numbers and in certain situations also the account numbers of the parties with whom they enter into such transactions.

The scope for extending the requirement of quoting the permanent account numbers to various types of transactions is very wide indeed, but in the interest of administrative efficiency it would be desirable to make only a small beginning and widen the field gradually. Legal provisions will also be necessary to make it obligatory for all permanent account numbers holders to intimate any change in their addresses to the appropriate authorities. The law will have also to provide penal measures for ensuring compliance.

However, for the present at least, it should not be obligatory for anyone to obtain an account number before entering into a transaction. The legal requirement should be that persons entering into specified transactions should quote their account number, if they have one. If they do not have an account number, they should be required to say so.

The law should require all persons carrying on business, where the turnover in a year is likely to exceed ₹ 30,000, to apply for allotment of permanent account numbers within the prescribed time—if they are not already taxpayers. The law may also provide that any subsequent change in the business name should be forthwith intimated to the concerned authorities. To save any hardship to the public arising out of delay in allotment of permanent account numbers, it could be provided that if a proper application for allotment of a number has been made within time, entering into transactions even before allotment of the permanent account number will not entail penal consequences.

Power of Survey: A new provision may be introduced as an adjunct to Section 133A of the Income Tax Act, 1961 to enable the income tax officer to visit any premises of an assessee for the purposes of counting cash, verifying stocks, and inspecting such accounts or documents, as he may require and which may be available there. He may also obtain any additional information and record statement of any person who is found at the premises, in respect of matters which would be relevant for making a proper assessment.

The law may be amended to confer powers of survey on the Inspecting Assistant Commissioners as well.

Increasing Survey Operations: Adequate number of survey circles should be set up to ensure comprehensive and continuing survey on rotational basis. Further, an officer of the rank of assistant commissioner should be placed in over all control of survey operation in each commissioner's charge and he should also hold charge of the special investigation branch. Besides, in the bigger cities like Delhi, Bombay, Calcutta and Madras, a survey range should be created under an inspecting assistant commissioner who will have a contingent of survey circle income tax officers and the necessary complement of inspectors under him. In other mofussil towns, the survey squad should be under the local inspecting assistant commissioner.

The income tax officer in charge of a survey circle should have territorial jurisdiction. It should be his responsibility to ensure that all persons having taxable income/wealth within his jurisdiction are brought on the registers of the Department.

The work relating to the first assessment in cases discovered on survey should be done by a separate officer or set of officers who will be entrusted solely with such cases. However, the assessing officers should not be under the assistant commissioner of income tax in charge of survey.

Collection, Collation and Dissemination of Information: The Central Board of Direct Taxes should lay down each year a programme and specify targets for collection, collation and dissemination of information. It should also ensure that the programme is strictly adhered to and efforts are made to reach the targets fixed. The sources to be tapped every year should be decided at the national level by the board at the beginning of each year, to be followed and implemented strictly at all levels. Different types of information may be collected in different years so as to keep an element of surprise.

With a view to securing efficient functioning of the set up, standards of work and performance should be laid down, without which it would not be possible to judge the requirements of manpower nor to measure the adequacy or otherwise of the output given by the persons at various levels. The special investigation branches, to be renamed as central information branches, should be suitably strengthened and they should be placed under the supervision of the Inspecting assistant commissioner in charge of survey operations. They should be located at the stations where the headquarters of the commissioners are but should not form part of their offices. The work of the special investigation branch should be inspected at least once a year by the commissioner of income tax himself.

Co-ordination between Banks and the Income tax Department: The legal provisions under which the system of p0ermanent account numbers is introduced should also include that tax payers should quote their permanent account numbers in applications for bank draft, mail transfers, telegraphic transfers, etc., if the amount involved in such transactions exceeds ₹ 5,000.

A suitably provision may be introduced in the Banking Regulation Act, 1949, by which all banking institutions coming within the purview of the Act should be under a statutory obligation to report to the Reserve Bank of India all financial transactions in cash over twenty-five thousand rupees which, in the judgment of the banking company concerned, are suspicious or unusual.

Officers of the department should be statutorily empowered to obtain from banks information of general nature, i.e., without reference to any particular taxpayer, provided the information that is sought is in respect of transactions over specified amounts.

Changes in the Form of Income tax Return: The form of return of income should be made more elaborate than what it is at present by incorporating a schedule of exempted income, net worth, personal expenditure and other outgoings.

To start with, the requirement to furnish this additional information should be applicable only when the total income exceeds ₹ 15,000.

A provision on the lines of Section 114 (1) of the Taxes Management Act, 1970 of U.K. which states that the validity of proceedings purported to be made under the taxing statute cannot be questioned for want of form or affected by reason of a mistake, defect or omission therein, may be incorporated in our direct tax laws as well.

Reintroduction of Expenditure Tax: Introduction of an expenditure statement as a part of the form of return of income should be quite effective in checking evasion through consumption expenditure, without disturbing the existing tax structure.

Uniform Accounting Year: Of the many provisions in the income tax law that provide scope for evasion and avoidance of taxes, the one which allows the tax payers to choose as many accounting years as there are sources of income is particularly noteworthy for its undesirable consequences.

The advantages that would accrue from the adoption of a uniform accounting year would far out-weigh the disadvantages. It will facilitate investigation and cross-verification of transactions and restrict the scope for collusive manipulations. White-washing of balance-sheets in collusion with one another will become difficult. Income earned during the same period by different taxpayers will be taxed at the same rate and not at different rates, as at present. Budgeting would be more accurate, for a boom or depression in a particular industry can be duly taken note of in the same year in case of all the assesses running that industry. It will also accelerate completion of assessments because economic conditions pertaining to a particular class of assesses would be common. Given sufficient time for the change-over, businessmen are also likely to get accustomed to it.

The Government should seriously consider the expediency of prescribing a uniform accounting year for all taxpayers. In that case, the accounting year should coincide with the budget year. In any event, the law should permit adoption of only one previous year', in respect of all business carried on by one person.

Checking Under-valuation of Immovable Properties: It would be expedient for the Government of assume powers to acquire immovable properties in cases of understatement of cost of construction as well. However, as this would be an extension of the recommendation in the interim report, the Government should consider such extension only after it has had some experience of acquisition of immovable properties in cases of understatement of sale consideration.

The Land Acquisition Act, 1894 may be amended to the effect that where an immovable property to be acquired under that Act, was the subject matter of a transfer within one year preceding the notification under Section 4 of the Land Acquisition Act, 1894, the sale consideration stated in the transfer deed to be the market value for the purpose of determining compensation under Section 23 of the Land Acquisition Act, 1894.

The suggestion for replacement of deduction in respect of repairs in computing the income from house property by depreciation is not favoured.

Ownership Flats: It may be provided by law that ownership flats, whether acquired through the medium of co-operative housing societies or otherwise, would be deemed to be immovable property for purposes of the Transfer of Property Act, 1882 and that transfer of such flats shall be required to be registered under the Indian Registration Act, 1980 in the same manner as any other immovable property.

***Pugree* Payments:** The present legislative control on rent which operates in respect of both residential and non-residential premises may be amended so as to restrict its operation to residential premises only.

Tightening Provisions of the Stamp Act: It will go a long way to help deter investment of black money in immovable property if adequate machinery is provided under the Stamp Act for valuation of properties which are the subject of transfer.

In 1967, the then Madras State Government had introduce certain measures to curb the evil of understatement of purchase consideration, by an amendment to the Indian Stamp Act, 1899. It would be advantageous to have similar machinery in other States also. The Indian Stamp Act, 1899 may be suitably amended in this behalf on the lines of the Madras enactment.

In addition to indicating the date of sale and name and address of the purchaser, the stamp vendors may be required to state on the stamped paper the purpose for which the paper was purchased and also the names of the parties to the transaction sought to be recorded thereon, except in the case of an agreement or a memorandum of agreement under Article 5 of Schedule I of the Indian Stamp Act, 1899 and power of attorney under Article 48 thereof.

Foreign Exchange Violations: An official study team appointed by the Government of India has estimated in its report recently submitted that the extent of leakage of foreign exchange is about ₹ 240 crore yearly. Since foreign exchange violations are possible only through clandestine dealings, these necessarily result in evasion o income tax and other allied taxes. It is understood that the Government is examining the report of this study team and is proposing to initiate necessary remedial measures in this regard, including certain amendments to the Foreign Exchange Regulation Act. It is expected that the appropriate authorities would deal with this matter effectively.

Tax Treaties for Exchange of Information Relating to Tax Evasion: Section 90 of the Income Tax Act, 1961 may be suitably amended to enable the Government to enter into agreements with foreign countries not only for the avoidance of double taxation of income buy also for prevention of fiscal evasion. Further, our existing agreements should be revised so as to provide for exchange of routine information and market intelligence as also specific information in individual cases to facilitate investigation of tax evasion and recovery of taxes. The agreements should also enable courts in both the contracting counties to entertain rogatory, commissions or letters of request from the tax authorities of the other country for the purpose of securing the evidence of persons resident therein. The agreements should further provide for mutual assistance in investigation of tax frauds and recovery of taxes by making the administrative machinery of each available to the other.

Tax Evasion in Film Industry: The law should be suitably amended to provide that where under an irrevocable annuity policy, though taken by the producer in his name but assigned in favour of the artiste, the remuneration is paid to the artiste in the form of an annuity spread over a number of years, the artiste should be taxed only on the amount of annuity received during the year. The present value of annuities due in future should be exempt from wealth tax. The producer would be entitled to claim the entire amount paid to the Life Insurance Corporation towards taking out such a policy as a deduction in the year of payment.

In view of the enhancement of the ceilings under clauses (ii) and (iv) of Section 80C (4) of the Income Tax Act, 1961 in recent years, the percentage of gross total income and the qualifying amount prescribed for artistes, playwrights, authors, etc., under rule 11A of the Income Tax Rules, 1962 should also be suitably enhanced.

Where the remuneration payable to an artiste under an agreement exceeds ₹ 5,000, both the film producer and the artiste should be under a statutory obligation to furnish a copy of the agreement to their respective income tax officers, within a period of one month from the date of execution of such an agreement.

Payment by Crossed Cheque or Crossed Bank Draft: An endeavour should be made to evolve a new instrument in the form of a bank bill of exchange which is readily transferable but also contains an obligation for it to be encashed through a bank account. A suitable pay order/draft of different denominations may be designed, and introduced for this purpose. In brief, this instrument should contain the following three essentials:

(i) that it is an equivalent of a pay order or draft, without the name of the payee at the time of issue;

(ii) that the name of the payee is entered on the instrument by the payer at the time of payment; and

(iii) that the instrument is marked 'account payee only' by the issuing bank so that it cannot be encashed except through a bank account of the payee. After the introduction of the new instrument as suggested above, the exceptions provided in rule 6DD of the income tax rules may be suitably curtailed.

***Hundi* Loans:** Permanent account numbers, which are to be assigned to the tax payers by the Department, should be statutorily required to be quoted on *hundi* papers. Further, advances of loans on hundi and their repayments, including interest, should be made through 'account payee' cheques only. This should serve as an effective check on bogus hundi loans.

Checking Tax Evasion among Contractors: In the case of contractors including sub-contractors, a register for recording daily receipts and payments would be essential and should be in a prescribed from in due course.

The income tax law may be amended to provided that payment to a sub-contractor will not be allowed as deduction in computing the taxable income of the contractor unless it has been made by an 'account payee' cheque.

The scope of Section 285A of the Income Tax Act, 1961 should be extended to apply to all contractors.

Contractors who have been penalised or convicted for concealment of income/wealth should not be awarded Government contracts for a period of three years. For this purposed, the form of tax clearance certificate applicable to contractors may be suitably amended to include information whether the contractor was penalised or convicted for concealment of income/wealth during the immediately preceding three years.

Blank Transfer of Shares: The existing provisions of the Companies Act with regard to the system of blank transfer of shares are not adequate to check misuse. The law may be suitably amended to provide that before an instrument of transfer is presented to the prescribed authority, the transferor should be required to state in the instrument itself his name, the distinctive numbers and value of shares proposed to be transferred, and the instrument of transfer should be duly signed by the transferor and bear the requisite stamp duty. The prescribed authority should be required to cancel the stamps on the instrument of transfer at the time of stamping or otherwise endorsing thereon the date on which it is so presented. The instrument of transfer should be valid for a period of two months only from the date of its presentation to the prescribed authority.

However, in order to protect the interest of genuine shares holders who want to borrow funds from banks on the security of shares, such blank instrument of transfer should be valid for the period the shares are held by the bank as security for an advance or overdraft to a registered shareholder.

***Benami* Investments:** In pursuance of the recommendation of the Administrative Reforms Commission, the Government has a sponsored legislation through the Taxation Laws (Amendment) Bill, 1971 to discourage *benami* holding of property. This is a step in the right direction.

Denial of Credit Facilities to Tax Evaders: All scheduled banks should be barred from providing credit facilities above ₹ 25,000 at any point of time to any person, unless he gives an affidavit to the effect that he has not been subject to any penalty or prosecution for concealment of income/wealth during the immediately pre ceding three years.

Tightening up Vigilance Machinery: Elsewhere in the report, recommendations have been given with regard to prevention of corruption among Government servants generally and in particular, views have been given on steps needed for prevention or detection and punishment of corruption in the income tax department. As regards the question of dealing with corruption at higher levels in public life and redressal of public grievances, the appointment of *lokpal* and *lokayuktas* after passage of the necessary legislation would take adequate care of the situation.

Arousing Social Conscience against Tax Evasion: Tax evasion cannot be tackled by stringent legal measures alone. It can be dealt with effectively only if such measures are backed by strong public opinion against black money and tax evasion. In helping to build up such public opinion, the Government can play a vital role. The foremost measure in this regard is denial of the privileges which are still available to tax evaders.

Tax evaders who have been penalised or convicted for concealment of income/wealth should be disqualified for the purpose of getting national awards. The law should also be suitably amended to disqualify such persons from holding any public elective officer for a period of six years. In addition, Ministers and senior officers of the Government should avoid, attending social functions sponsored or organised by known tax evaders.

A person who has been penalised or convicted for concealment of income/wealth should not be eligible to be a director of a limited company for a period of six years. The Companies Act, 1956, may be amended accordingly.

Tax education should be imparted in our schools as part of a course in civics.

Lists of taxpayers published by the Government should include figures of income declared, income assessed and the tax payable. Such lists should, in addition to being published in the official gazette, be publicised in local papers and be also put up on notice boards in income tax officers.

The Chambers of Commerce and the Federation of Chambers should take the lead and evolve methods by which businessmen resorting to corrupt trade practices, including tax evasion, are ostracised.

Taxpayers who have been filing correct returns and have been prompt and regular in meeting their tax obligations should be treated by the department as starred assesses.

Tax Avoidance

Introductory: In an acquisitive society, it is more common for a taxpayer to regard taxation as a burden and to seek all possible means to escape it. The distinction between 'evasion' and 'avoidance' is largely dependent on the difference in methods of escape resorted to. Some are instances of merely availing, strictly in accordance with law, the tax exemptions or tax privileges offered by the Government. Others are manoeuvres involving an element of deceit, misrepresentation of facts, falsification of accounts, including downright fraud. The first represents what is truly tax planning, the latter tax evasion.

However, between these two extremes there lies a vast domain for selecting a variety of methods which, though technically satisfying the requirements of law, in fact circumvent it with a view to eliminate or reduce tax burden. It is there methods which constitute 'tax avoidance'.

Attempts at tax planning or methods such as availing of the various benefits and concessions provided under the tax laws should not be shunned as unethical or anti-social. But those types of tax avoidance which violate the spirit and intention of the law and at times border on tax evasion are certainly disapproved.

Concept of Taxable Income: Income tax statute should contain a comprehensive definition of income whereby all incomings are brought to tax, subject to specified exemptions provided therein.

Casual and Non-recurring Receipts: The exemption now available to the casual and non-recurring receipts under the Income tax Act should be withdrawn. The following scheme of taxation of receipts of casual and non-recurring nature is suggested:

(i) Receipts which are of a casual and non-recurring nature and are in excess of ₹ 1,000 in a year should be included in the total income to be taxed at normal rates. Reasonable expenses should be allowed. Exemption up to ₹ 1,000 would relieve the taxpayer of the responsibility to account for petty receipts.

(ii) Winnings from State lotteries may be taxed on a concessional basis as applicable to long-term capital gains on assets other than lands and buildings.

(iii) Casual losses should be set off only against the same type of income. For instance, losses in respect of racing would be set off only against income from racing.

(iv) Tax @ 33 percent should be deducted at source from prizes in crossword puzzles, race winnings and lotteries and where the amount exceeds ₹ 1,000.

Capital Gains: Capital gains should not be treated on a par with other income. Such gains may be partly attributable to inflationary pressures and, in any case, represent income which has accrued over a period of time. Concessional treatment of capital gains should apply only to capital assets held for more than five years. Accordingly, the definition of short-term capital asset will have to be changed.

Hindu Undivided Family (HUF): HUF as a unit of assessment is retained in most cases only when it enables the persons concerned to reduce their tax liability and in other cases, it is promptly partitioned without considerations of sentiment coming in the way. HUF should be taxed at a special rate if any of its members has independent income above the maximum not liable to tax. Such HUF should be taxed at the following rates:

Income (₹)	Rate (percent)
5,001-10,000	15
10,001-15,000	25
15,001-20,000	35
20,001-30,000	45
30,001-50,000	55
Over 50,000	65

In addition, 15 percent surcharge should also be leviable where the income exceeds ₹ 15,000.

Similarly, under the Wealth Tax Act, there should be a separate schedule with higher rates applicable to Hindu undivided families where any member of family has independent wealth above the exemption limit.

Clubbing Income of Husband, Wife and Minor Children: Family consisting of husband, wife and minor children being treated as a unit of assessment is not favoured.

Measures to Check Diversion of Income: Clause (v) of Section 64 (1) of the Income Tax Act, 1961, should be suitably amended by introducing a deeming provision, if necessary, to cover income arising from assets transferred indirectly.

Section 64 (1) of the Income Tax Act, 1961 should be suitably amended, to provide that in computing the income of a parent-in-law or a paternal grand parent, there shall also be included such income as arises directly or indirectly through assets transferred by him/her directly or indirectly otherwise than for adequate consideration to or for the benefit of a daughter-in-law or a minor grandchild, as the case may be.

By a suitable Explanation to Section 64 (1) of the Income Tax Act, 1961 the effect of the judgement of the Supreme Court in the case of *Commissioner of Income Tax vs. Prem Bhai Parekh and others* (77 I.T.R. 27) should be taken away.

It should be provided in law that in computing the total income of an individual there shall be included all such income as a arises directly or indirectly to the spouse of such individual by way of salary, commission, fees or any other form of remuneration from a concern in which such individual has substantial interest. For this purpose, an individual may be deemed to have a 'substantial interest': (a) in the case of a limited company, if its shares carrying not less than 20 percent of the voting power were, at any time during the previous year owned beneficially by such individual either singly or along with his relatives, and (b) in the case of any other concern, if such individual either singly or along with his relatives was entitled in the aggregate at any time during the previous year, to not less than 20 percent of the profits of such concern. For this purpose, the term 'relative' should have the same meaning as in clause (41) of Section 2 of the Income Tax Act, 1961.

Tax Treatment of Firms and Partners: The Partnership Act should be so amended as to preclude the admission of minor to the benefits to partnership. However, in order to avoid hardship, an exception may be made in the case of succession on the death of a parent. Further, until such an amendment is made to the Partnership Act, the Income Tax Act should be amended to provide for inclusion of a minor's share from a firm in the income of that parent whose total income is higher.

Claims of sub-partnerships should be investigated in depth to uncover collusive arrangements.

Where a partner in a firm is an undisclosed benamidar of an outsider, and any one or more of the other partners knew or had reason to believe that it was so, the firm should not be treated as a validly constituted partnership.

The levy of a separate tax on registered firms rendering professional services should be discontinued.

Share Dealings by Companies: The results of dealings in shares by companies other than investment, banking and finance companies, should be treated in a manner analogous to speculation business.

Treatment of Perquisites: The Government should re-examine all the existing rules pertaining to valuation of perquisites in order to update them with reference to the current market trends.

Taxation of Discontinued Business: A provision on the lines of Section 176 (4) of the Income Tax Act, 1961, should be added to cover also income from business received after its discontinuance.

Charitable and Religious Trusts: Every person in receipt of income derived either from property held under trust or other legal obligation for charitable or religious purposes or from voluntary contributions received on behalf of such trust or institution should be required to furnish a return of income if the total income, ignoring the exemption under Section 11 and 12 of the Income Tax Act, 1961 exceeds the maximum amount not chargeable to income tax.

The law may be amended to provide that where a person, who is under an obligation to furnish a return of income under Section 139(4A) of the Income Tax Act, 1961, fails to furnish such a return, he shall be liable to pay penalty up to one percent of the income of the trust for each year of default or part thereof.

The income tax law may be amended to cast an obligation on all charitable and religious trusts which seek income tax exemption to register themselves either the Income tax Department. Trusts which fail to get registered within a prescribed period will not be entitled to claim income tax exemption. The existing trusts may be required to get themselves registered within one year from the date of enactment of the new provision and trusts formed after the enactment of the new provision and trusts formed after the enactment should get themselves registered within six months of the date of the constitution of the trust.

All trusts with incomes/receipts exceeding rupees twenty-five thousand should be under a statutory obligation to have their accounts audited in the prescribed manner.

Law should be suitably amended to provide that where a trust for the relief of the poor, education or medical relief derives income from any activity for profit, its income would be exempt from income tax only if the said activity for profit is carried on in the course of the actual carrying out of a primary purpose of the institution. So far as trusts for any other object or general public utility are concerned, pursuit of any activity for profit should continue to render them ineligible for tax exemption.

The existing conditions for spending the trust income for charitable purposes within the same year, or accumulating it in the specified manner, should be relaxed, where the trust is prevented from complying with them on account of not having actually received from the income in question.

All 'ghost' or anonymous donations to charitable trusts should be taxed at the rate of 65 percent. Religious trust may, however, be left out of the purview of this provision.

Where any part of the corpus or income of a charitable or religious trust is used by or for the benefit of the founder, trustee, etc., for any period in a year, such a trust should be liable to pay wealth-tax on the value of its entire property in the same manner as the discretionary trusts under the provisions of Section 21 (4) of the Wealth Tax Act, 1957.

Barring the original corpus, there should be a total ban on trusts investing any of their funds in any business concern, including a limited company.

Section 13 of the Income Tax Act, 1961 provides, *inter alia*, that a charitable or religious trust or institution will be denied exemption from tax if the funds belonging to it are invested, or continue to remain invested, during the previous year in any concern in which the author or founder thereof or substantial contributor to it or their relative has a substantial interest. This condition should not operate when such an investment itself forms a part of the initial corpus of the trust.

The term 'substantial portion' used in Section 13 of the Income Tax Act, 1961 should be so defined as to mean any property or income exceeding one thousand rupees and the term 'substantial contribution' used in the said Section should be defined as an amount exceeding five percent of the corpus of the trust. Further, persons mentioned in Section 13(3) of the Income Tax Act, 1961 should also include a trustee and his relatives and the term 'relative' should also include relatives through marriage.

Section 12 of the Income Tax Act, 1961 may be amended to provide that the benefit of tax exemption in respect of income received by way of voluntary contributions will be available only to charitable and religious trusts which ensure wholly for the benefit of the public. Further, it may be provided that the voluntary contributions received by religious and charitable trusts will be treated as income of such trusts for the purpose of Sections 11 and 13 of the Income Tax Act, 1961. However, voluntary contributions in the nature of endowments or for specific projects related to the objects of the trust may be allowed to be accumulated or set apart.

The law may be suitably amended to provide that exemption under Sections 11 and 12 of the Income Tax Act, 1961 will be available to trusts created before April 1, 1962 if they conform to the requirements of the law as applicable to trusts created after March 31, 1962. The period for effecting the necessary changes may be fixed at two years from the date of amendment of the law in this behalf. As some mixed trusts may have to be split up for this purpose, a suitable machinery may be set up by the Government to effect a smooth change over.

There is a strong case for having an all-India legislation for the purpose of controlling and regulating the working of various public charitable and religious trusts in India. Apart from the provisions contained in the draft Bill, which was introduced in the Parliament in 1968 for this purpose (but which lapsed with the dissolution of the Lok Sabha in 1970), such legislation should contain some further provisions. The Government should have the power to nominate one or more trustees in the case of a trust with income exceeding ₹ 50,000 per annum, notwithstanding the terms of the trust deed. There should also be a provision against the continuance of the same persons as trustees on the governing body of a trust. The number of life trustees in any public trust should not exceed 25 percent of the total strength of its trustees. As regards other trustees, the principle of rotation should be introduced so that one-third retire every five years. No trustee should be eligible for re-appointment more than once. Further, there should be yet another provision to ensure that the number of trustees who are close relatives of the founder(s) of a trust, does not at any time exceed 25 percent of the total strength of the trustees. These provisions should be made applicable even to the existing trusts.

Measures to Check Avoidance of Wealth Tax: Sub-clause (iii) of clause (a) of Section 4 (1) of the Wealth Tax Act, 1957, (which corresponds to clause (v) of Section 64 (1) of the Income Tax Act, 1961 should also be amended to cover indirect transfer of assets.

There is another type of diversion where a parent-in-law or paternal grandparent transfers assets directly cr indirectly, otherwise than for adequate consideration, to the daughter-in law, or minor grandchild, as the case may be, for his or her immediate or deferred benefit. A suitable provision may be made in the Wealth Tax Act for the inclusion of the value of such transferred assets in the net wealth of the parent-in-law or paternal grandparent, as the case may be.

In the matter of valuation of unquoted shares, the wealth-tax rule in this behalf tilts the scale in favour of the shareholder. According to this rule, the value is determined, subject to certain adjustments on account of dividends declared, with reference to the book value of the assets and liabilities as reflected in the balance sheet. This rule completely bars revaluation of immovable properties held as assets by the company.

It is common knowledge that closely-held companies downing huge immovable properties in big cities show only the depreciated value of such properties in their balance sheet though their market value is, in fact, several times the book value. The position in this behalf should be reviewed, and for the purposes of valuation of shares of closely-held companies, the rule should be revised to provide revaluation of immovable properties held by such companies—other than as their business premises—so as to bring the value of such properties up to their fair market value, taking into account, *inter alia*, their actual yield.

The valuation of immovable properties once adopted after due enquiry should remain unchanged for a period of five years, except for additions, alterations and improvements. Any change in the basis of levy of wealth tax from 'market value' to 'cost price' of an asset is not favoured.

Bibliography

Bibliography

A.R. Prest, *Public Finance in Theory and Practice*, London: Weidenfeld and Nicolson, 1970.

Administrative Reforms Commission, *Report of the Study Team on Centre-State Relationships*, Volume I, 1968.

Alan Peacock and Francesco Forte (eds.), *The Political Economy of Taxation*, Basil Blackwell, Oxford, 1981.

Durga Das Basu, *Introduction to the Constitution of India*, New Delhi: Prentice-Hall of India Private Ltd., 1987.

G.S. Sahota, *Indian Tax Structure and Economic Development*, Asia Publishing House, Bombay, 1961.

Government of India, *Report of the Indian Taxation Enquiry Committee*, 1924-25, Volume I, (President: Charles Todhunter).

—*Report of the Income Tax Investigation Commission* (Chairman: Srinivasa Varadachariar), 1948.

—*Report of the Taxation Enquiry Commission* (Chairman: John Matthai) 1953-54, Volumes I, II and III.

—*Report of the Customs Reorganisation Committee,* (Chairman: F.C. Budhwar), 1957-58.

—*Report of the Direct Taxes Administration Enquiry Committee* (Chairman: Mahavir Tyagi), 1958-59.

—*Report of Central Excise Reorganisation Committee* (Chairman: A.K. Chanda), 1963.

—*Report of the Committee on Sales Tax* (Chairman: R.G. Saraiya), 1964.

—*Final Report on Rationalisation and Simplification of Tax Structure* (Chairman: S. Bhoothalingam), 1968.

—*Final Report of Direct Taxes Enquiry Committee* (Chairman: K.N. Wanchoo), December 1971.

— *Report of the Committee on Taxation of Agricultural Wealth and Income* (Chairman: K.N. Raj), 1972.

——*Report of the Central Excise (Self-Removal Procedure) Review Committee* (Chairman: B. Venkatappiah), 1973.

——*Report of the Indirect Taxation Enquiry Committee* (Chairman: L.K. Jha), 1977, Part I.

——*Report of the Indirect Taxation Enquiry Committee* (Chairman: L.K. Jha), Part II, January 1978.

——*Final Report of Direct Tax Laws Committee* (Chairman: C.C. Chokshi), 1978.

——*Report of the Expert Committee on Tax Measures to Promote Employment* (Chairman: V.M. Dandekar) 1980.

——Economic Administrative Reforms Commission, *Report on Tax Administrations*, 1981-83.

——*Report of the Expert Committee on Replacement of Sales Tax by Additional Excise Duty* (Chairman: Kamlapati Tripathi), January 1983.

——Central Board of Excise and Customs, *Guide to MODVAT.*

——*Aspects of the Black Economy in India,* March 1985.

——*Long Term Fiscal Policy* (December, 1985).

——*Report of the Technical Study Group on Central Excise Tariff* (Chairman: J. Datta), Part I, 1985.

——*Study Group on Taxation of Expenditure* (Final Report), 1987.

——*Report of the Commission on Centre-State Relations* (Chairman: R.S. Sarkaria), 1988, Part I.

——*Interim Report of the Tax Reforms Committee* (Chairman: Raja Chelliah) December 1991.

——*Final Report of the Tax Reforms Committee* (Chairman: Raja Chelliah) Part I, 1992.

——*Advisory Group on Tax Policy and Tax Administration for the Tenth Plan* (Chairman: Parthasarathi Shome), 2001.

——*Report of the Task Force on Direct Taxes* (Chairman: Vijay Kelkar), December 2002.

——*Report of the Task Force on Indirect Taxes* (Chairman: Vijay

Kelkar), December 2002.

—*White Paper on State-Level Value Added Tax* (Chairman: Asim Kumar Dasgupta), 2005.

—*Rationalisation of Customs and Excise Duties on Edible Oils and Oilseeds* (Chairman: Ashok Lahiri), 2006.

—Ministry of Finance, *White Paper on Black Money*, May 2012.

—Ministry of Finance, *Budget Papers* (various years).

—Ministry of Finance, *Economic Survey* (various issues).

—*Reports of Finance Commissions.*

—Planning Commission, *Five Year Plans.*

—Ministry of Law and Justice, *Constitution of India.*

Institute of Fiscal Studies, *The Structure and Reform of Direct Taxation*, Report of a Committee Chaired by Professor J.E. Meade, London: George Allen and Unwin, 1978.

J.A. Kay and M.A. King, *The British Tax System,* Oxford University Press, 1978.

J.F.J. Toye (ed.), *Taxation and Economic Development*, London: Frank Cass and Company.

James Cutt, *Taxation and Economic Development in India*, New Delhi: Vikas Publications, 1969.

M.M. Sury, Sales Tax in India Since 1938, *Journal of the Indian School of Political Economy*, Volume 7, No. 1, January-March 1996.

—Tax Structure Developments in India: 1950-90, *Journal of the Indian School of Political Economy*, Volume 3, No. 1, January-March 1991.

Nicholas Kaldor, *Indian Tax Reform: Report of a Survey*, Government of India, Ministry of Finance, 1956.

Reserve Bank of India, *Report on Currency and Finance* (various years).

—*Bulletins.*

—*Occasional Papers.*

Richard Aronson, *Public Finance*, New York: McGraw-Hill Book Company, 1985.

Richard Bird, *Taxation and Development*, Harvard University, 1970.

Richard M. Bird and Oliver Oldman (ed.), *Readings on Taxation in Developing Countries*, The Johns Hopkins Press, Baltimore, 1967.

Richard Musgrave and Peggy Musgrave, *Public Finance in Theory and Practice*, New York: McGraw-Hill Book Company, 1989.

R.W. Bahl, *Tax Revenue Forecasting in Developing Countries: A Conceptual Analysis*, IMF, DM/72/83.

Simon James and Christopher Nobes, *The Economics of Taxation*, Oxford: Philip Allan, 1978.

V.G. Rao, *The Responsiveness of Tax System in India*, New Delhi: Allied Publishers Pvt. Ltd., 1979.

Vito Tanzi, 'The Impact of Macroeconomic Policies on the Level of Taxation and the Fiscal Balance in Developing Countries', *IMF Staff Papers*, Volume 36, No. 3, September 1989.

Walter Mahler, *Sales and Excise Taxation in India*, New Delhi: Orient Longman Ltd., 1970, p. 154.

Index

Index